·I Want to Know™· *About* GOD, JESUS, THE BIBLE, and PRAYER

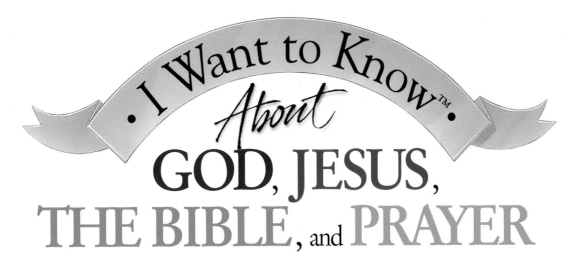

I Want to Know™ *About* GOD, JESUS, THE BIBLE, and PRAYER

Rick Osborne and K. Christie Bowler

Zonderkidz
The Children's Group of Zondervan Publishing House

Heritage Builders™

For Lightwave
Concept and Direction: *Rick Osborne*
Managing Editor: *Elaine Osborne*
Text Director: *K. Christie Bowler*
Questions and Activities: *Kevin Miller*
Art Director: *Terry Van Roon*
Desktop Publishing: *Andrew Jaster*

Scripture portions taken from the *Holy Bible, New International Reader's Version* Copyright © 1994, 1996 by International Bible Society.

Contributing Artists:
Lillian Crump—pp. 38–39, 76–77, 114–115, 152–153
Gerard DeSooza—pp. 29, 34, 50, 51, 56, 63, 90, 91, 98–100, 109, 113, 146, 148, 149
Gustave Doré—pp. 71, 147
Chester Goosen—Photos on pp. 21, 31, 40, 57, 75, 78, 88, 104, 105, 116, 126, 133, 134, 154
Andrew Jaster—pp. 53, 55, 129
Chris Kielesinski—pp. 14, 15, 24, 29, 34, 36, 37, 50, 52, 56, 58, 59, 61, 63, 68, 73, 89, 90, 91, 98–100, 107, 109, 111, 112, 128, 132, 136, 139, 145, 146, 149
Ken Save—pp. 14, 17, 20, 30, 54, 72, 95, 96, 127, 137, 144
Rod Sawatsky—pp. 13, 18, 31, 53, 62, 69, 92, 93, 101, 103, 108, 130, 131
Emilios Shiatas—Airbrushing on pp. 29, 34, 50, 51, 56, 63, 90, 91, 98–100, 109, 112, 146, 149
Ed Strauss—pp. 23
Terry Van Roon—pp. 19, 32, 74, 151

Photos on pages 11, 19, 26, 27, 28, 35, 49, 60, 69, 70, 87, 90, 94, 103, and 125, courtesy of Zondervan Publishing House.

Photo on page 16 courtesy of NASA.

The images used on pages 12, 13, 22, 24, 25, 27, 33, 127, 131, 132, 140, 141, 142, 143, 150, and 151 were obtained from IMSI's Master Photo Collection, 1895 Francisco Blvd. East, San Rafael, CA 94901-5506, USA.

This edition is printed on acid-free paper.

Zonder**kidz**™
The Children's Group of Zondervan Publishing House

Published by Zondervan Publishing House, Grand Rapids, Michigan 49530, U.S.A. http://www.zondervan.com

Printed in Singapore.

All rights reserved.

LIGHTWAVE
building Christian faith in families
Lightwave Publishing Inc. www.lightwavepublishing.com

00 01 02 / TWP / 5 4 3 2 1

Contents

I want to know about . . . God

God the Creator 12
He Made It; He Cares; Desert Master.

12

God Is Real 14
How Do We Know God Is Real?; He Designed It; He's the Source of; Better and Best.

God Is Awesome 16
He's Everywhere; He Knows Everything; He Can Do Anything; It Affects Us; A Hamster-Eye View.

The Only God 18
The One and Only; Three In One; Three Persons, Three Jobs.

He Made Us 20
Made by the Best; Made Like the Best; Children of the Best.

We Chose Poorly 22
A Bad Choice; Homeless; Made for Family; Consequences and Judgment.

Results of the Fall 24
Lies and Rumors; Wrong Thoughts of God; What Happened?

Various Religions 26
Beliefs About God; Buddhism; Hinduism; Islam.

Jesus Shows Us God 28
Behind-the-Scenes Cause; Love in a Body; Jesus Shows Love; Jesus Is God.

Jesus Saves Us 30
A-Mazing; The Way Was Death; Walking Through; A Salvation Prayer.

Growing with God 32
Begin the Adventure; Relationship; God's Goal; Help Along the Way.

What Is God Like? 34
What a Person!; What a Character!; God's Character Sketch.

You Are God's Best!

20

I want to know about . . . **Jesus**

52

70

I want to
know about . . . **The Bible**

96

102

How to Use This Book

Congratulations on purchasing this book! Teaching your children the basics of the Christian faith, such as the truth about God, Jesus, the Bible, and prayer, is one of the most valuable things you can do for them. It's not easy to find the time or creativity to do this job effectively, but this book is full of interesting articles, challenging questions, and entertaining games, puzzles, and activities that will make this task a breeze.

Making the Most of It

Before you get into the book, there are a few things you should know that will help you and your children get the most out of your learning times together.

Alone or Together: All of the questions and activities in this book have been designed so that children can either work through them on their own or with a parent or older sibling's help. You and your children can decide whether they should use this book as a supplement to their personal devotional time or if it is something you want to work on together. Some of the activities require more than one person, but for the most part your children can do them alone.

Photocopy It: Some of the activities, such as fill-in-the-blanks, multiple choice, word searches, and so on, make it look like you can write the answers right into the book. But before you do that, consider photocopying these exercises instead. That way your book stays neater, and you are able to use it with more than one child. Perhaps you can get your children to keep their pages together in a special notebook or binder so that they don't lose their hard-won knowledge.

Keep It Regular: Consider setting aside a weekly or daily time for your children to work through this book. This will ensure that they are constantly learning exciting new facts about God, Jesus, the Bible, and prayer. It will also provide you with an excellent opportunity to discuss these issues each day or each week with your children. Go with a system that suits your family and your children's unique personalities.

Step-by-Step: Rather than have your children read through the entire book first and then do all of the related exercises and activities, have them read one section per day or per week and do the exercises immediately afterward. This will ensure that the material covered by each set of exercises is still fresh in your children's minds and that they are not overwhelmed with information when it comes time to do the exercises.

Get Excited: Remember, if you are excited about learning, your children will be excited about it as well. A good idea is for you to read through the articles and exercises beforehand yourself so that you are prepared to walk through the material with your children. If there are any aspects of the material that you think your children will have questions about, do a bit of research so you are ready for their questions. The more you put into these lessons, the more you will get out of them.

Make It Fun: Above all, make learning about these topics a fun experience for everyone. Learning is good, but we learn best what we enjoy the most. People have been turned off of the Christian faith simply because their first exposure to it was boring and uninspired. Look for ways to spice up the learning times so that your children will begin to associate learning about God with fun and excitement. One way to enhance these learning times is to follow them up with a scrumptious snack, a family discussion, a game, a movie, or some other activity that your children enjoy.

A Note on the Activities

The interactive pages in this book contain three different types of questions and activities. The first set of questions, "Learn It," tests readers on what they learned. These questions are not meant to be comprehensive. For example, many of the fill-in-the-blank questions will have more right answers than the number requested. The goal of these questions is merely to get children to review the material and reinforce what they have read. The second set of questions, "Think About It," helps readers to see how what they have just read applies to their lives. It also gives them an opportunity to respond to the material in a personal way. The third set of activities, "Do It" or "Play It," adds a fun element to the learning process with games and puzzles that help readers remember and apply what they've read.

The questions for each topic are grouped at the end of each section rather than interspersed throughout the chapters. For example, all of the questions on God are at the end of the section that covers God. Most answers can be found directly in the text itself. However, we have provided answers to the multiple-choice questions, the fill-in-the-blanks, and some of the games and activities that require answers that are not obvious from the text. These answers can be found at the end of each section of questions. We haven't provided answers for questions that involve application or personal response from the reader because they will vary widely from child to child.

Are you ready? Gather your kids and go for it!

I Want to Know™

About GOD

God the Creator

He Made It

Breathe deeply. Feel the air fill your lungs—air with the right proportions of the right gases to keep you alive. On a clear night, look up—millions of stars! Listen—frogs croak, crickets sing! Every part is important: stars, air, insects, tides. . . .

What makes galaxies spin? What causes insects to pollinate flowers at the right time? How do salt's two poisonous chemicals become something we can't live without? How did Earth become perfectly balanced, perfectly placed, perfectly inhabited? The questions are endless.

And the answer is God! He planned and created everything ideal for life. In fact, if any of thousands of details were different there would be no life! God made the immense universe with galaxies so huge we can't imagine them and atoms so small we'll probably never see them.

Creation is incredible! But not as incredible as its Creator!

He Cares

How can such an amazing God have time for us? Easy. We're why he made it all! We're front and center in his mind. If he takes care of life's details for his creatures, providing nests for birds, perfect beaks for hummingbirds to get nectar, and air bladders for fish to swim, he'll take care of us. We're more important to him than birds and fish!

God's creation shows us God. "Ever since the world was created it has been possible to see the qualities of God that are not seen. I'm talking about his eternal power and about the fact that he is God. Those things can be seen in what he has made" (Romans 1:20).

- *God loves balance.* Earth is the right distance from the sun to support life. Our atmosphere has the right proportions of gases.

- *He cares.* He provides everything that makes life possible. Plants turn the sun's light into food. Bacteria help us digest.

- *He keeps things in order.* God made the world work by rules to keep us safe—gravity makes things fall, light travels in straight lines.

- *He's trustworthy.* The HUGE universe and our small planet are in his hands.

- *No detail is too small for him.* Each creature is perfectly designed for its environment—hunting leopards blend into the trees, mussels' super-glue keeps them safe from waves.

- *He's intelligent.* We think and learn. It takes someone intelligent to make someone intelligent.

- *He gave us rest.* Creation goes in cycles—night/day, winter/summer, work/play.

In the beginning God created everything and put all the details in place. Creation makes it clear there is a God behind it all. Who is this God? What is he like? What does that have to do with us? Let's find out!

Desert Master

God specially engineered the one-hump dromedary for the desert. They're:

Perfectly Sand-Proof:
- Long eyelashes and inner eyelids keep sand out.

- Stretchy hooves prevent sinking.

- Nostrils close partway to keep out sand and let air in.

Perfect Water Users:
- Their eighty-pound hump is full of fat to use when there's no water.

- After losing 225 pounds in eight days without water, a ten-minute drink of twenty-seven gallons brings them back to normal.

- Blood reduces from 94 percent water to 60 percent without harm. (If our blood goes to 82 percent water, we die!)

God Is Real

How Do We Know God Is Real?

Have you ever seen, tasted, or smelled God? Is he real? Does it make sense to believe in God? Think about this: Have you ever tasted or smelled love? No. Is it real? Absolutely! We know love is real because we see what it does: kind acts, hugs, forgiveness, smiles, acceptance. In the same way, looking at what God has done helps us know God is real. That's why we can learn about him from what he made.

Think about these things and see if they don't help you know God is real.

He Designed It

Look around. Notice anything? Objects fall down. Trees grow up. With heat, water boils and wood burns. The sun rises every day. The world is predictable and orderly. It follows a design so well that scientists can make rules about it! Is this chance? Not likely! That's like saying the *Mona Lisa* painting was made by a paint spill. NOT! Just as someone painted Mona Lisa, someone designed the world: God.

He's the Source of ...

Intelligence: You're reading this. You can think. Ever wonder how you do that? Thinking is complicated. Where did it come from? Someone thought up thinking and made the world an intelligent place. That someone is God, the first thinker and source of thinking.

The God idea: Throughout history people have believed in God or gods. Where did that idea come from? Why is it everywhere? God put it into us. He built us to know he's real!

Conscience: If you tell a lie or are mean, you probably feel bad. Your conscience tells you that you did something wrong. How do you know some things are right and others wrong? Your parents taught you some of it, but they couldn't give you a conscience. No, it came from the one who made right and wrong: God.

Beauty: We live in a beautiful world! Sunsets, flowers, faces, paintings, scenery. We enjoy beauty—think of our response to newborn kittens or rainbows. But beauty doesn't do anything. Something doesn't have to be beautiful to work. So why have it? Who would make something nice for no reason except enjoyment? God would!

"Foolish people say in their hearts, 'There is no God'" (Psalm 14:1). Think about it. Look around and ask questions about what you see, why it's there, or why it works the way it does.

Eventually your questions will lead you back to the ultimate answer: God. He's definitely real! He has to be for us to have a world to live in and think about.

Better and Best

Here's something to get your head around: Why do we think one thing is better than another? We think a multispeed mountain bike is better than a tricycle. A vacation is better than staying home. A poor but happy family is better than a lonely rich person. Where do we get the standard of better and best? No matter what we think of, we can usually think of something better. But eventually, somewhere there has to be an ultimate BEST that beats out everything else. Somewhere there is something or someone that *nothing* can be better than: God.

God Is Awesome

He's Everywhere

God is real. He has always been and always will be. We know he's spirit (he has no physical body), but what's he *like?* Can we know? Yes! Nature teaches general things about God. But God wants us to know him in detail. He gave us a book, the Bible, that tells us what he's like, how life works, and more.

Look in the mirror. You're not a shapeless blob oozing out into endless space. You have limits; you fill a certain space and have edges separating you from your surroundings. Everything has limits. Except God. The Bible tells us God is *omnipresent*—present everywhere. He fills the universe. Go anywhere—God is already there! "Who can hide in secret places so that I can't see them? . . . Don't I fill heaven and earth?" (Jeremiah 23:24).

He Knows Everything

You know things and you learn more every day, at school and at home.

Everyone learns. Not God. He's *omniscient*—he already knows everything, from what you like for breakfast, to how to make a planet, to what unborn people will do.

Everywhere you go your knowledge goes. You can't take out bits, like how to add, and stick them in the hamper with your dirty shirts. They're part of you. God can't be somewhere without his knowledge either. Everything he knows is everywhere he is.

"The Lord knows what people think. . . . There is no limit to his understanding. . . . He even counts every hair on your head! . . . Nothing God created is hidden from him. His eyes see everything" (Psalm 94:11; 147:5; Matthew 10:29–30; Hebrews 4:13).

He Can Do Anything

Can you do whatever you want? Can you fly or breathe under water? Nope. You don't have the power. In fact, you can't even make yourself taller! But God can do *anything* and *everything* he wants. He's *omnipotent*—all-powerful. He spoke and the universe was created! "Great is our Lord. His power is mighty. . . . You have made the heavens and the earth. Nothing is too hard for you. . . . With people that is impossible. But with God, all things are possible" (Psalm 147:5; Jeremiah 32:17; Matthew 19:26).

It Affects Us

We have limits: stops and starts, beginnings and ends. But God doesn't. That's great! You see, who God is affects us. Because he's everywhere, we're never alone. Because he can do anything, he can help with any problem. Because he knows everything, including what's best for us, he can give us perfect advice. God told us these things about himself so we'd know we can trust him.

A Hamster-Eye View

Two hamsters look outside their cage and argue about whether what they see (you) is real. They can't touch or understand you—you're so much bigger than they are—so they decide you're not real. Silly, huh? They decide what's real by their understanding and experience. But they don't have all the information to make a good decision. Even if they did, it wouldn't make sense to them. But no matter what they do or don't know, you're still real.

Like hamsters, we don't have all the information about God. And some of what we do know is hard to understand. But it would be silly to decide God can't be real just because we can't figure him out!

The Only God

The One and Only

There are no other gods besides God. Think about it: If you made a whole village out of play dough, would there be things in it you didn't make? No way. In the same way, since God made everything in the universe, it's impossible for creation to contain anything God didn't make. So there can't be some other "god" out there somewhere. Besides, if God fills everything (which he does), where would other "gods" live? There's no place for them.

"I am the one and only God. Before me, there was no other god at all. And there will not be any god after me. . . . I am the First and the Last. I am the one and only God. . . . There is no other god" (Isaiah 43:10; 44:6; 46:9).

Three in One

One bike. What happens if you take the bike apart? No more bike—only parts of a bike. One means a whole. God is one. You can't divide him into parts. Everything God is, he is all the time. His qualities, like omnipresence, are part of his *nature*, they make him who he is. At the same time, the Bible says God is three! Look at Jesus' baptism (Matthew 3:16–17). Jesus the *Son* was in the water. The *Spirit* came down like a dove. And the *Father* spoke from heaven. God is three persons—Father, Son, and Holy Spirit. God is all three at the same time, and they're all one God! They're not parts of God. All three share the same nature—they all fill everything, know everything, and can do everything. Therefore they're one God. So what makes them three? Their persons and their jobs.

Think about it like this: Imagine your best friend and you have no bodies. You both fill everything (including each other). You both know everything (including each other's thoughts), and you both can do anything. In almost every way you and your friend would be the same—two-in-one. Only two things would make you different from each other: your personalities and what you decided together you would each look after or be responsible for. You would be two persons sharing one nature.

Three Persons, Three Jobs

The Father: Source and creator of everything. "He is the Father. All things come from him" (1 Corinthians 8:6). He sent his Son. Jesus said, "The Father who sent me . . ." (John 5:37).

The Son, Jesus Christ: Died to save us from our sins. "While we were still sinners, Christ died for us" (Romans 5:8). He will judge us. "The Father . . . has given the Son the task of judging" (John 5:22). He prays for us. "Christ Jesus is . . . praying for us" (Romans 8:34).

The Holy Spirit: He's with us. "[God] will give you another Friend to help you and to be with you forever. The Friend is the Spirit of truth" (John 14:16–17). He helps, teaches, and grows us to be more like Jesus. "He will teach you all things. He will remind you of everything I have said to you" (John 14:26). "Salvation comes through the Holy Spirit's work. He makes people holy" (2 Thessalonians 2:13). He gives us gifts. "Different kinds of gifts . . . are all given by the same Spirit" (1 Corinthians 12:4).

The dove is a symbol of the Holy Spirit.

People use different pictures to understand how God is three in one.

He Made Us

Made by the Best

God made everything. But why make us?

Say you're alive forever and can do absolutely anything. What would it be? Fly around for ninety years? Play ball for sixty? Seriously, how would you spend your time? God must have thought about it because he decided to do something incredible! He made the universe, filled it with galaxies, planets, stars, and black holes. Then he made life on Earth. He made all kinds of living things: microscopic critters, maple trees, crabs, dolphins, puppy dogs and ants, lions and kangaroos. He made oceans, mountains, rivers, deserts, and forests. He made everything around us. Then he made something different from everything else: people!

Have you ever wondered what makes you different from your pet dog, gerbil, or fish? Well, you talk. You wear clothes, ride a bike, and go to school. But the real difference is in how we were made.

Made Like the Best

God, the Best, made us like himself—like God! We're made in his *image*. God is different from us, true, but in some ways we're like him:

God is spirit: We have spirits. Our spirit makes us alive. A body without a spirit is just skin and bones. Our spirits will live forever with God when this life is over.

God knows and God does: Like God, we have minds that let us learn and know things. We think and plan. We have wills that let us choose. We act and make things happen.

God is in charge of everything he made: He's responsible and does what he promises. He gave us responsibilities too—to take care of the world and each other.

God has emotions: He feels love, anger, grief, and joy. Like God, we get upset or feel joy. We laugh at a good joke or just because. We love our family and friends, and we feel their love for us.

Children of the Best

Why did God interrupt his peaceful existence to make the universe? Why make you and me? Because he wanted someone to love, and he wanted to be loved by us. God wanted a family, so the Father, Son, and Spirit made a family of humans. The plan was that God would pour out all his love onto this human family, and we would pour out our love on him. We would love him, obey him out of trust, enjoy his company, and receive his incredible love.

God wanted to care for us, protect us, guide us, teach us, and help us be more like him so that we can be the best possible people and have the best possible lives. He made us because he is love. He planned for us to be together as the best and closest family ever. "Father, I pray that all of them will be one, just as you are in me and I am in you. I want them also to be in us" (John 17:21). "How great is the love the Father has given us so freely! Now we can be called children of God. And that's what we really are!" (1 John 3:1).

You Are God's Best!

God created everything. Can you find Adam and Eve, the first people? How many animals are in the picture?

We Chose Poorly

A Bad Choice

This Father/child relationship with God sounds great! What happened? The first people ruined it!

Say you have a pile of fruit to choose from. God tells you the orange striped one will kill you and change the world forever. No orange striped fruit for you! But what if someone says, "Aw, it won't kill you. It'll make you really smart!" Now what? Just a nibble? That's what happened to the first people, Adam and Eve. They ate the forbidden fruit and wrecked everything.

Why did God let them? He loved them. He wanted their love to be given back freely. That means Adam and Eve had to be able to choose *not* to love God. And that's what they did. They didn't trust him. They went their own way, which is sin, instead of trusting God's love. That choice ruined the relationship for everyone who came after them. Bad choice!

Homeless

Imagine running away from home: Nowhere to sleep. No food or shelter. Did your parents want you to be cold and hungry? No. Your parents want to care and provide for you. *You* made the choice to run away. God wants the best for us too. That best means being part of his family. He wants to care for us and make sure we have everything we need and then some. His plan is to love us as his children. But we (through Adam and Eve) ran away from home.

Made for Family

God created relationships as a wonderful blessing in our lives—relationships with him and with each other. "God said, 'It is not good for the man to be alone. I will make a helper who is just right for him'" (Genesis 2:18). We were made for family. That's God's gift to us.

Some may think it's not fair that God made us need him. That's like saying it's not fair that we have to eat. Was God mean to make us need food? Of course not. In fact, he made food wonderful! God made chewy pizza and mouth-watering chocolate. He made food to bless us.

That's how relationships should be—a pleasure. God made us to need him and each other because it's good for us. Loneliness was never in the plan. Friendships make life good. But a good relationship with God makes it even better! Adam and Eve wrecked their relationship with God when they chose sin. To get back into God's family, we have to return to God.

Satan, disguised as a snake, told Eve the fruit would make her like God.

Consequences and Judgment

CRASH! One broken vase. And one big punishment! Why do your parents discipline you? They're trying to help you become wise and mature. They forgive you, but there are consequences: you pay for the vase. The world works by consequences: play with fire and you get burned; lie and people will stop trusting you.

God made the world to work in certain ways that match who he is. When we trust God and do things his way, life works better. When we don't do them his way and sin instead, things go wrong. Sin has consequences.

God doesn't want to be our judge. He wants to be our Father. He corrects and teaches us for our sake.

Adam and Eve disobeyed God and ate the fruit.

Results of the Fall

Lies and Rumors

Ever since Adam and Eve chose not to have a relationship with God, people have gotten wrong and weird ideas about what God is like and who he is. They began to think he was different than he was. They stopped believing he was a loving Father. Satan (who told Adam and Eve God was wrong and the fruit wouldn't hurt them) spread lies about God.

When a relationship breaks, we no longer know the other person well. It's easy to believe lies about them.

Wrong Thoughts of God

It wasn't long before people were making up untrue things about God and how the world works. They started believing the lies and teaching them as if they were true. **But** in the Bible, God tells us the truth about the world and himself. Take a look at these false beliefs about God. Then look at what God says:

Agnosticism: believes there's no way to know if God is real. Agnostics think faith, believing without proof, is foolish. They say you cannot know for sure. It's "I don't knowism." **But** the Bible says,

"Faith is being . . . certain of what we do not see. . . . Without faith it isn't possible to please God. Those who come to God must believe that he exists" (Hebrews 11:1, 6).

Atheism: believes there is no God. End of story. The universe just happened. **But** the Bible says, "Foolish people say in their hearts, 'There is no God'" (Psalm 14:1).

Pantheism: believes God didn't make the universe; the universe *is* God. Nature is another name for God.

You're as much God as an oak tree, a beaver, or a star. **But** the Bible tells us God created things different from himself. "In the beginning, God created the heavens and the earth" (Genesis 1:1).

Pluralism: believes there are many right ways to God. People can believe whatever they want. It all leads to the same place. They say Jesus isn't the way to God. In fact, it's wrong to tell people he is. **But** Jesus made it very clear and simple, "I am the way and the truth and the life. No one comes to the Father except through me" (John 14:6).

Polytheism: believes there are many gods responsible for different parts of life. Some are more important or powerful than others. Some are evil. People can become gods. **But** God said, "I am the one and only God. . . . There is no other god" (Isaiah 46:9).

What Happened?

Adam and Eve's bad choice affected *everything!*

Death and separation from God: God is life. Sin separates us from God. Being separated from life means death—in our spirits and bodies.

Pain: We have sickness, pain, and sadness. We hurt each other. People lie, blame, get angry, and are mean. Our bodies and hearts hurt.

Hard work: We work hard just to eat and have clothes and houses.

Nature is dangerous: Thorns and thistles scratch. Snakes are poisonous. Predators kill. Bacteria cause diseases. Mosquitos bite!

The world groans: Things decay and rot. Our planet is in bad shape. "We know that all that God created has been groaning. It is in pain" (Romans 8:22).

Various Religions

Beliefs About God

When you don't know someone it's easy to make up things about them. People who didn't know God came up with beliefs about him and taught them as true views of God. Does that make them true? No. The truth is always the truth no matter what we think about it. The Bible says God is truth. If we really want truth, we'll find God.

Here are some false beliefs:

Buddhism

About 2500 years ago a man believed he found *enlightenment* or true knowledge. He became *Buddha* and taught:

(1) Life is suffering. (2) We suffer because we want things. (3) To avoid suffering, stop wanting! (4) To stop wanting, have right thinking, goals, efforts, speech, behavior, actions, understanding, and meditation. This leads to life's goal, *nirvana*, where we become nothing. We have no souls. We keep being reborn into new lives until we reach nirvana.

Buddhists believe God is pure nothingness. But God is a person. He says, "I AM WHO I AM" (Exodus 3:14).

Hinduism

From a worm to a god! Hinduism says this can happen:

(1) There are many gods, but they're all *Brahman*. (2) Only *Brahman* is real—the universe isn't really here. (3) *Brahman* is the eternal soul or god. Life's goal is to realize *we* are *Brahman*. (4) We do this through living good lives. We have many! We might start as worms. If we're good worms, we might be reborn as birds. Eventually, if we're good, we're born as humans. (5) There are four *castes* or classes of people. We start at the

bottom (as laborers) and move up to priests by living each life well. Once we've been good priests, we're united with the eternal soul, *Brahman*.

Hindus believe God has no personality. But God says, "I am a God who is tender and kind. I am gracious. . . . slow to get angry. . . . faithful and full of love. I continue to show my love to thousands of people. I forgive those who do evil. . . . who refuse to obey . . . and who sin" (Exodus 34:6–7).

Islam

About 1400 years ago, a man named Mohammed said he had a revelation from God or *Allah*.

Five Beliefs: (1) There's only one God. (2) The chief angel is Gabriel. Shaitan is a fallen angel. (3) The scriptures are the Koran (Mohammed's ideas) and some parts of the Bible. (4) There are twenty-four prophets, including Jesus. Mohammed was the greatest. (5) Allah will judge the dead.

Five Duties: (1) Become a Muslim by publicly saying, "There is no god but Allah and Mohammed is his prophet." (2) Pray five times daily toward the city of Mecca. (3) Give gifts to the poor. (4) Fast in daytime during the Muslim month of Ramadan. (5) Visit the temple in Mecca. These things save you.

Muslims believe that only strict obedience to Islamic laws matters to God. But the Bible says love matters. "Suppose I can understand all the secret things of God and know everything about him. And suppose I have enough faith to move mountains. If I don't have love, I am nothing at all. Suppose I give everything I have to poor people. . . . If I don't have love, I get nothing at all" (1 Corinthians 13:2–3).

Jesus Shows Us God

Behind-the-Scenes Cause

How do we find out who God really is? We read the Bible and look at Jesus!

Why do you buy candy? Because you're hungry or just for fun? Your reason is your *motivation*, your behind-the-scenes cause. We have different motivations for what we do. Imagine having the same motivation for every single thing! God does. His one motivation is *love*.

Think about this: you're human. You can't do anything that's not human—say, make food from sunlight or breathe oxygen under water. In the same way, God is love! He can't do anything that's not loving.

Love in a Body

Picture love as a person. What would she look like? Blonde? Chubby and jolly? Stop! Love *is* a person. Love looks just like God. If you're not sure

that helps, get this: God became a person like you and me. His name was Jesus Christ. He came to show us what love looks and acts like. "How did God show his love for us? He sent his one and only Son into the world" (1 John 4:9).

God sent Jesus, his Son, to live among us as a human. God is loving and unselfish. He wanted to give to us. Even with the relationship broken, God never stopped loving us. "God loved the world so much that he gave his one and only Son" (John 3:16). Jesus came to show us God. Like a lion, he is strong and fierce. He will protect us. And like a lamb, he's gentle and humble. He's the "Lamb of God [who] takes away the sin of the world" (John 1:29).

Jesus was Love in a body.

Jesus Shows Love

While Jesus lived here, people saw, touched, and heard God. Jesus was God made visible. "Christ is the exact likeness of God, who can't be seen" (Colossians 1:15). Here's what Jesus showed us. God:

Cares about our pain: Jesus healed the sick and brought dead people back to life. He cried with people and helped those in pain and trouble.

Looks after our needs: Jesus fed people and gave to the poor.

Helps us know the truth: Jesus taught about God and preached the great news of his love.

Welcomes us: Jesus welcomed all kinds of people and let them hang around him, including children, lepers, sinners, the rich, and the poor.

Is kind: A sinful woman everyone looked down on approached Jesus. He let her wash his feet with her tears and dry them with her hair. And he forgave her sins.

Read more about Jesus in the Bible's Gospels: Matthew, Mark, Luke, and John.

Jesus Is God

Here are verses that tell us Jesus is God:

God's voice from the cloud said, "This is my Son, and I love him. I am very pleased with him. Listen to him!" (Matthew 17:5).

"I and the Father are one. . . . When they look at me, they see the One who sent me. . . . If you really knew me, you would know my Father. . . . Anyone who has seen me has seen the Father" (John

10:30; 12:45; 14:7, 9).

"God was pleased to have his whole nature living in Christ . . . in human form" (Colossians 1:19; 2:9).

"The Son is the gleaming brightness of God's glory. He is the exact likeness of God's being" (Hebrews 1:3).

Jesus Saves Us

A-Mazing

Jesus helped us understand who God is again. He opened the way and brought us back to the beginning, to God's intention to be our Father!

Ever been stuck in a maze? Dead ends everywhere. No matter which way you turn or how many paths you try, you're stuck. It's frustrating and possibly frightening. Help!

Life can be like a maze. People keep looking for ways to reach God. Many, like the Buddhists, Hindus, and Muslims, think they've found it. But they've found only dead ends.

God made the way for us—he sent his Son. Jesus lived as one of us to show us what God is like by how he lived and acted. He came so we'd know he can understand us—our temptations and problems. Finally, he lived with us—to die for us!

The Way Was Death

Jesus lived to die!

Sin wrecked the relationship and still separates us from God. It puts a big dead end between us and all the paths we try to take to get to him.

"Everyone has sinned. . . . When you sin, the pay you get is death" (Romans 3:23; 6:23). Since we all sin, we all deserve to die. But God had a plan. If someone without sin was willing to die in our place to pay for our sins, God would accept that payment. He would forgive us, and we could have that great Father/child relationship with him. No more dead ends!

That's exactly what Jesus did! He lived without sin. He was innocent, but he paid for our sins by dying a horrible death on a cross. His friends put his body in a tomb, but that wasn't the end. No way! On the third day he was alive again! He reached right through all the dead ends and opened the way to relationship with God again.

Walking Through

Now instead of a dead end there's a clearly marked way that says, "To God." It's open to everyone who (1) believes Jesus is God's Son, (2) admits they're a sinner who needs forgiveness, (3) accepts that Jesus paid for their sins, (4) asks God to forgive them, be their Lord, and live in them, and (5) with God's help, lives as God wants.

Jesus is the way through the maze! We don't have to try to find God. God came to us! "Jesus answered, 'I am the way and the truth and the life. No one comes to the Father except through me'" (John 14:6). We're saved and alive forever! "But God gives you the gift of eternal life because of what Christ our Lord has done" (Romans 6:23).

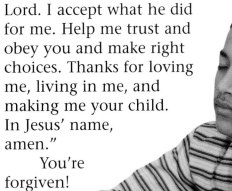

A Salvation Prayer

If you haven't accepted Jesus yet and you want to be God's child, pray this prayer: "Dear God, I know I'm a sinner. I've made wrong choices and done bad things. I'm sorry. Please forgive me. I know your Son, Jesus, died for my sins. I believe you raised him from the dead, and he is Lord. I accept what he did for me. Help me trust and obey you and make right choices. Thanks for loving me, living in me, and making me your child. In Jesus' name, amen."

You're forgiven! Party time!

Growing with God

Begin the Adventure

Yahoo! We're back with God! Now what? Do you make the track team and stop running? No way! Making the team is the beginning! Next come the fun and the work. Being a Christian (God's child) is the same. We become a Christian and the fun begins!

Now that we have our Father/child relationship with God back, we need to start doing things his way, like Jesus did. God is now our Father who guides, teaches, protects, and watches over us as he has wanted to. And we learn how to be his children by talking to him, and trusting and obeying him.

Relationship

"Continue to work out your own salvation. . . . God is working in you" (Philippians 2:12–13). Ever try to have a relationship with someone who didn't want one? Relationships take two. God works on it with us. We get to know people by talking and sharing our hearts with them. It's the same with God. We spend time getting to know him by reading his book, meeting his other children, and talking to him in prayer.

And we obey him. Jesus said, "If you love me, you will obey what I command" (John 14:15). God wants us to obey him because he loves us. Remember, he knows everything. He knows the best way to live and what will make us happy.

God's Goal

Why does God want this relationship with us? It's the whole purpose of creation! Talk about important! God made us to love and be with. It's hard to imagine that someone would want our love so much they'd make a universe, wait hundreds of years, and die to get it! But that's

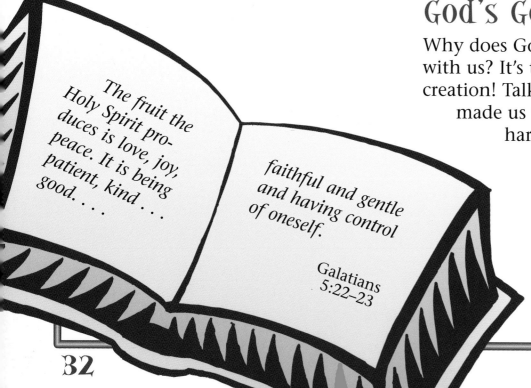

The fruit the Holy Spirit produces is love, joy, peace. It is being patient, kind . . . good. . . . faithful and gentle and having control of oneself.

Galatians 5:22–23

Help Along the Way

The Bible: God gave us the Bible to help us know him. It's his love letter telling us about himself. It's also the instruction manual for a good life. When it says "Don't lie," that's because God knows lying hurts us. The Bible teaches us truth. It corrects and trains us in what's right. (See 2 Timothy 3:16–17.)

Prayer: Relationships are built through communication. We communicate with God through prayer. Prayer involves sharing our hearts with God. Also, through prayer we ask for what we and others need. God says if we come to him, he'll be glad to answer.

The Church: You're not the only Christian. You're part of a huge family! It's important to join a church, a group of God's children. In church we learn about God, grow together, and help each other. The church also helps the poor and tells others about God.

exactly what God did. He wants to care for us better than the best dad, guide and teach us more than the most knowledgeable teacher, protect us better than the greatest warrior, and encourage and cheer us on more than the best friend. That's why he made us.

As our relationship grows, we'll find almost without noticing it that we start to resemble Jesus. We become people others like to be with. We see God's fruit in our lives. "The fruit the Holy Spirit produces is love, joy, peace. It is being patient, kind . . . good. . . . faithful and gentle and having control of oneself " (Galatians 5:22–23).

Celebrate!

What Is God Like?

God can do anything. He saved his people by making a dry road through a sea!

God is the only god. In a challenge with the followers of a fake god, God's fire burned up the altar.

God is faithful. When Daniel was punished for obeying God, God kept him safe. He shut the lions' mouths.

What a Person!

Who is this God we're getting to know? In some ways he's similar to us.

What's your personality? Friendly, quiet, adventurous, studious? These qualities—your likes, attitudes, and quirks—make up your personality. You're a complicated person! Did you know God has personality? He is full of personality! And all of God's qualities, likes, attitudes, and quirks are perfect, *infinite*, and without limits. It boggles the mind!

What a Character!

Our character is the quality that guides what we do and how we live. God has great character! He is:

Good: God gives as much goodness as people can handle. He puts others first. Jesus healed the sick and fed the hungry. He even died so his enemies could be forgiven! God acts good because God is good. And he'll be good to us. Count on it!

Honest and Truthful: God is always the same, no matter what. How God acts is who God is. He is truth! He can't lie, tell part truths, say things he doesn't mean, or pretend to be someone he isn't.

Loving: Warm, fuzzy feelings. Hugs. Kind words. Acceptance. These say "love" to us. Love is treating people gently, with respect. It's wanting to be with them and wanting the best for them. God *is* love. Everything he does comes out of love—including discipline. God's love knows what's best for us.

Merciful: Remember how you're disciplined when you get in trouble? You probably deserve it. But sometimes we don't get what we deserve—we get mercy instead. Mercy is undeserved kindness, patience, and forgiveness. God knows what we've done and why. But he doesn't give us what we deserve. He's infinitely merciful. We can come to him without fear even when we've done wrong.

Perfect in Character: Look through a window on a sunny day, and you'll see smudges. The sun shows them up. God is like a pure, clean, glass window—no sun will ever show smudges on him! He's holy. That means there's nothing bad in him at all. He's perfect! Perfectly good, perfectly true, perfectly loving, perfectly merciful. There will never be the tiniest wrong in God.

All this means we can trust God. He's always the same. And he loves us. He wants to bless, care for, and be close to us. And he always acts toward us according to his character.

God is like a merciful father. He always welcomes us.

God's Character Sketch

"Lord, you are good. You are forgiving. You are full of love for all who call out to you" (Psalm 86:5).

"The Lord is good. His faithful love continues forever" (Psalm 100:5).

"The Lord . . . is kind and tender. . . . He is faithful and right in everything he does. All his rules can be trusted. . . . He is faithful and honest" (Psalm 111:4, 7–8).

"God is spirit" (John 4:24).

"The One who promised is faithful" (Hebrews 10:23).

"Every good and perfect gift is from God. It comes down from the Father. . . . He does not change like shadows that move" (James 1:17).

"God is love" (1 John 4:16).

And God said, "I have loved you with a love that lasts forever. I have kept on loving you with faithful love" (Jeremiah 31:3).

God Is Faithful

Unchanging God

God sounds great! But what does that mean for us? Lots!

Imagine that one day gravity quits! You'd have to grab something quick, or you'd float away! Without gravity you'd never come back to Earth. But don't worry, you can count on gravity. Wherever there's a large mass, like Earth, there's gravity. Always. We build our lives around the fact that gravity will keep doing its thing.

God *made* gravity! He's way more consistent than it is. "I am the Lord. I do not change" (Malachi 3:6). "[The heavens] will pass away. But you remain" (Hebrews 1:11). God never changes. We can build our lives around *that* fact. God's character will always be God's character. More than gravity, God is always the same.

Trustworthy, Faithful God

We can trust someone when we know their character and that they care about us and can help us. We know God's character and love for us means he'll always act with our best in mind. We can trust him. We don't even have to think about it! He's *trustworthy!* We can trust God with our lives because we know his

way is the best way and will make our lives better.

Once we trust someone, we need to know he can do what we're trusting him for. We need to know that when he says he'll do something, he will, no question. God will. He's *faithful.* We can put our faith in God and rely on him to do what he said he would do as our Father: look after us and help us grow.

God spoke to Moses through the burning bush. Moses trusted God to lead him.

Noah obeyed God even when he didn't understand. And God saved him.

Timeless Love

Love isn't just touchy-feely warm fuzzies. God's love is strong. He's there for the long haul. He cares who you are now and who you'll become. He sees your whole life and knows how to make you into the best person you can be. He doesn't pop into your life for a day, give an order, then take off for months. No way! He's with you all the time. He cares about every part of your character and life. He wants you to be a loving, respected person and, later, have a good job, strong friendships, and a solid, loving marriage.

All that takes a God who's always the same, always faithful, who cares about both the details *and* the big picture. That's exactly who God is! We can count on his love! Absolutely.

Faith Test

God knows exactly what he's doing. Sometimes when bad things happen, it doesn't *feel* like God loves us. Maybe we move to a school where we can't find friends. It's hard to feel God's love. What's going on?

Look at the big picture. What's more important—our relationship with God and his plan for our lives and growth, or a quick fix? Sometimes, for our sakes, God lets things happen because he knows what we need to become the best possible us. "Your troubles have come in order to prove that your faith is real. It is worth more than gold" (1 Peter 1:7). No matter what, one thing never changes: God loves us. Even though we may not understand what is happening to us, God is working out everything for our good. That's as solid as rock, as certain as gravity.

Great Big God

God is so big that we've barely begun to find out who he is in this book. No matter how much we get to know him, there's always more to learn. We'll never get bored with God as our Father and friend!

Q   Who created God?

A   No one created God—he has always existed. We can't understand this because everything that we know has a beginning or an end. Each day has a morning and night; basketball games have an opening tip-off and a final buzzer; people are born, and they die. But God has no beginning or end. He always was and always will be.

Q   How and why did God create the world?

A   Whenever we make something, like a craft, a drawing, or a sand castle, we have to start with special materials, like clay, string, glue, paper, crayons, and sand. We can't even imagine creating something out of nothing—by just saying the words and making it appear. But God is so powerful that he can do what is impossible for us. That includes making anything he wants, even creating things from nothing.

JASON'S IMAGINATION

That's what it means to be God—he can do anything.

God created the world and everything in it because he enjoys making things, and he wanted to be with us. God created people because he wanted to have friends, men and women, boys and girls, with whom he could share his love. He created the world for them to live in and enjoy.

Q How does God make the sun and moon go up and down?

A God made powerful laws to govern the universe. These laws control the movements of the sun, moon, earth, and other planets and stars. For example, one law called "gravity" draws objects toward each other. Other natural laws control the weather. Many forces determine whether the day will be sunny or cloudy, warm or cold, such as the heat from the sun, the currents in the ocean, the wind, and many others. God set up the rules that make all these forces work together. And because God controls the entire universe, he can interrupt the laws if he

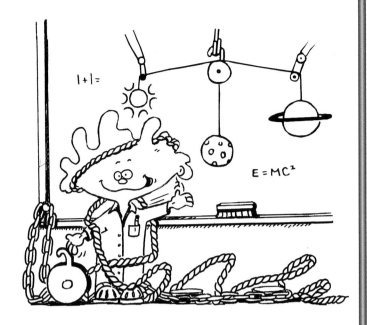

wants to—bring rain to dry land or bright sunshine to flooded areas. How powerful God must be to control all that!

Q Would God send nice people to hell if they are not Christians?

A Compared to each other, some people are nice and some are

mean. But compared to God, all people are not very good. All people need to be forgiven for their sins, not just "mean people." To be fair, God has to punish sin. God doesn't want to send anyone to hell. That's why he sent Jesus—to pay the penalty for our sins by dying on the cross. But, unfortunately, not all people are willing to admit that they sin and ask for forgiveness. They don't accept the payment of Jesus' death for them. So God lets them experience the result of their choice.

Adapted from *101 Questions Children Ask About God*, Tyndale House Publishers, 1992. Used by permission.

Put It All Together

Big Dreams

What would make you the happiest kid in the world? Having scientists prove that eating junk food is good for you? Having your own plane to fly all around the world? Having a huge toy store to share with your friends? What is the greatest blessing you could have? The true happiness key—the blessing that will last forever and fill you to-the-brim full of joy—is what this book is all about: a relationship with the God who made and loves you! With God by your side, life can't get any better!

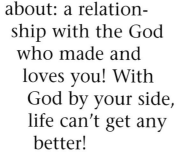

Our Hero

We all have heroes: movie stars, athletes, musicians. Imagine meeting your hero and hanging out with him or her! What a privilege!

God is the greatest hero of all. Being able to hang out with and get to know him is the greatest privilege of all. Relationship with him isn't a requirement or something we ought to do. It's an awesome chance to know the greatest hero of all time. God has invited us not just to hang out with him for a short time, but to be with him always! Wow! Talk about a privilege!

God knows us inside and out, and he loves us. He enjoys spending time with us.

When we started this book, we looked at the stars and saw God in what he made. We learned about who he is by looking at what he made and what the Bible said. Now we're setting out on a journey to get to know him the best possible way: personally! When we take God up on his invitation, we'll find he becomes more and more real to us.

Let's seek this incredible God and have the greatest happiness!

Questions and Activities

Pages 12–15

Learn It

1. Name three things creation shows us about God:

   _____,

   _____,

   _____.

2. What are four ways we can know that God is real?

   _____,

   _____,

   _____,

   _____.

3. If God made everything, then who made God?
   a. We did.
   b. No one made God. His mother gave birth to him.
   c. No one made God. God has always existed and will always exist.
   d. Einstein traveled back in time and made God in the year 1,000,000 B.C.

4. What has it been possible to see since the creation of the world? (Hint: Read Romans 1:20.)

   _____,

   _____.

Think About It

1. Think about something you've made and are proud of—such as an art project, a homemade card, or a meal. How did you feel about that project after you created it? You are God's project. How do you think he feels about you?

2. When did you first realize that God was real? What brought you to that conclusion? What do you think life would be like if God wasn't real? For example, if God wasn't real there would be no one to help us with our big problems, or we wouldn't know when one thing was better than another thing. What else would be different?

3. How should knowing that God created the world affect the way we treat the environment? What are three things you can do this week to help care for God's creation?

Do It

1. On page 13 we showed you how perfectly engineered one-hump dromedaries, or "Desert Masters," are for their environment. God made them complete with special eyelashes, stretchy hooves, and an emergency water supply system. What other animals can you think of that God has created so that they are perfectly suited to their environments? The following three are good examples. The eagle is an "Air Master." The dolphin is an "Ocean Master." And the penguin is a "Polar Master." Do a bit of research on these animals in an encyclopedia or on the Internet. See if you can come up with five aspects of each creature that make them perfectly suited to where they live.

EAGLE

_____ ,

_____ ,

_____ ,

_____ ,

_____ .

DOLPHIN

_____ ,

_____ ,

_____ ,

_____ ,

_____ .

PENGUIN

_____ ,

_____ ,

_____ ,

_____ ,

_____ .

Pages 16–19

Learn It

1. Put these words into the correct blanks below: _omnipresent, omnipotent, omniscient._

GOD IS

_____
(all-powerful)

_____
(everywhere)

_____
(all-knowing)

2. How many Gods are there?

_____

3. Why is there only room for one God in the universe?

_____

_____ .

4. What are the names of the three persons who together are God?

_____ ,

_____ ,

_____ .

How are these persons the same?

_____ .

How are they different?

_____ .

Think About It

1. If God is all-knowing, all-powerful, and present everywhere, why do you think he cares about us? How does knowing that God is all of these things affect the way you pray to him?

2. What do you think things would be like if there was more than one God? Do you think it is good that there is only one God? Why or why not?

Do It

1. On page 17 we talked about some foolish hamsters who decided that because they couldn't touch or understand the people outside their cage the people

weren't real. Sometimes humans behave like those hamsters. We think that because we can't see, touch, or completely understand God, he isn't real. That sort of thinking is foolish because there are many things in life that we can't see, touch, or understand, and yet we accept that they are real. Can you think of any? See if you can come up with five invisible things in the world around you. We've included some hints below to help you out.

Hint #1: Flick on a light switch. What happens? What makes this happen?

Hint #2: Turn on your radio. What do you hear? What makes this happen?

Hint #3: Go look at your fridge. Are there any notes, photos, or pictures attached to the front of it? What holds them there?

Hint #4: Step outside. Look at the tops of the trees. Are they moving? What makes this happen?

Hint #5: Pick up a shoe, lift it high above your head, then let go of it. What happens? What makes this happen?

2. Imagine that God allowed you to be omnipotent, or all-powerful, for one day. What would you do? Rearrange the continents so that your home was in the tropics? Bring back the dinosaurs? Give yourself a life span of 1,000,000 years? Write a one page story describing what that spectacular day would be like. Once you're finished, share your story with your parents, your siblings, or a friend.

Pages 20–23

Learn It

1. What are four ways in which people are similar to God?

_____,

_____,

_____,

_____.

2. How was God's relationship with his people ruined?

_____

_____

_____.

3. How does this broken relationship affect your life today?

_____

_____

_____.

4. What is sin? What are some consequences of sin?

_____

_____

_____.

Think About It

1. Why do you think God created us? Why do you think God created you?

2. How should knowing that other people are children of God affect the way you treat them? What are three things you can do this week to show people in your family, or your church family, that you and God love them?

3. Think of a time when you disobeyed God. How did you feel afterward? What were the consequences? How do you think God felt about what you did? What did you do to try to make things right?

Play It

1. God is given a lot of names in the Bible to describe different aspects of his character and nature. How many names of God can you think of? Try and unscramble the following names of God. What does each of them tell us about God? If you get stuck, look up the verse below each name to find the answer.

    a. AFREHT
       (Matthew 5:16)

    b. BABA
       (Mark 14:36)

    c. HTE DORW
       (John 1:1; 1:14)

    d. ULROENWDF UOLCNREOS
       (Isaiah 9:6)

    e. HSREPDEH
       (Isaiah 40:11; Jeremiah 31:10)

    f. OKCR FO EALSIR
       (Genesis 49:24)

    g. GIKN OF GINSK
       (Revelation 19:16)

    h. RDOL FO SDROL
       (1 Timothy 6:15)

    i. NICPER OF AEPEC
       (Isaiah 9:6)

    j. GIHH SEIRPT
       (Hebrews 6:20)

    k. HPLAA NAD GOAME
       (Revelation 22:13)

Pages 24–27
Learn It

1. Who do wrong thoughts about God come from?

    _____,

    _____.

2. Match the following belief systems with their definitions below.

    _____ Pantheism

    _____ Polytheism

    _____ Agnosticism

    _____ Atheism

    _____ Pluralism

    a. The belief that there is no way to know if God is real
    b. The belief that there is no God
    c. The belief that everything is God
    d. The belief that there are many ways to God
    e. The belief that there are many Gods

3. Buddhists believe that God is:
    a. everywhere
    b. a man named Siddhartha Gautama
    c. a colorful, four-winged bird
    d. pure nothingness

4. Hindus believe that the goal of life is to:
    a. accept Brahman as their savior
    b. realize we are all Brahman
    c. serve Buddha
    d. praise Allah

5. Muslims believe that:
    a. only strict obedience to Islamic laws matters to God
    b. Jesus was an angel
    c. there are only two gods: Gabriel and Shaitan
    d. Allah is a woman

Think About It

1. How do the versions of God presented by other religions compare to the God we read about in the Bible? Are they better or worse? Why do you think this is?

2. Have you ever heard a bad rumor about someone that you later found out was untrue? How did you feel when you found out the truth? Did that rumor damage your relationship with that person? Why or why not? What can you do to make sure that you don't get led astray by rumors?

3. How many different religions can you name? See if you can come up with 10. Why do you think there are so many religions?

4. Different religions spread a lot of bad rumors about God. Can you name five false rumors about God spread by different religions? What effect do these rumors have on people who don't know God? How can you help others not to be led astray by false rumors about God?

Pages 28–31

Learn It

1. What is God's single motivation for doing anything?

   _____,

   _____.

   Why can't God ever do anything that is unloving?

   _____,

   _____.

2. Who is "Love in a Body"?

   _____.

What are three ways he shows God's love to us?

_____,

_____,

_____.

3. What is the penalty or payment for sin?

   _____.

   Who paid the penalty for us?

   _____.

   How did he do this?

   _____

   _____

   _____.

4. Put these steps to salvation and following God in their proper order:

   _____ a. live as God wants, with his help

   _____ b. accept that Jesus paid for your sins

   _____ c. believe Jesus is God's Son

   _____ d. admit you're a sinner who needs forgiveness

   _____ e. ask God to forgive you, be your Lord, and live in you

Do It

1. Have you accepted Jesus as your Lord and Savior? If so, write a one page story describing how that decision came about. How has your life changed since then? If you haven't accepted Jesus, talk to someone you know who has, and write a one page story about his or her experience. How has this person's life changed since then?

2. *Put Yourself in the Picture*

In this section we compared God's coming as a person to the earth he created to an artist entering his or her own painting. It sounds impossible, but nothing is impossible with God. To help remind yourself of what God did for us, do the following activity.

Get out a sketch pad and some colored pencils. Think of the most beautiful scene you can imagine. For some people it may be the beach, for others it may be a meadow in the woods. Once you've decided on your scene, draw a picture of it in your sketch pad. Leave enough room on the bottom to write the verse: "I have come that they may have life, and have it to the full" (John 10:10).

After you've completed your picture, ask your parents if you can have a recent photograph of yourself. (You'll need to cut it, so make sure it's okay for you to keep it.) Once you have your photograph, take some scissors and trim away the background until you're the only person left. Now, find a place in your picture where you would like to see yourself resting or having a good time, then put yourself in the picture by glueing or taping the photo to your picture.

You've done it! You're in the picture. This is something like the way God came into his "picture," the earth, to give us life to the fullest. Only God didn't just put a picture of himself on earth, he really came into the world as a three-dimensional, living, breathing, eating, sweating, working human! Put your picture up on your bedroom wall as a reminder of this wonderful thing God has done for you.

Pages 33–35

Learn It

1. List three reasons why it's important to go to church:

   _____,

   _____,

   _____.

2. What are *two* ways of describing the Bible?
   a. God's grocery list
   b. God's instruction manual
   c. God's day-timer
   d. God's love letter

3. Why does God want to have a relationship with us?
   a. He's just being nice so he can borrow some cash
   b. He's lonely
   c. He needs some slaves to do his dirty work for him
   d. He created us and he loves us as his children

4. What are three results of the growth of our relationship with God?

   _____,

   _____,

   _____,

Think About It

1. List five elements of God's character. In what ways is your character like God's character? In what ways is it different? What are some ways you can develop godly character?

2. Have you ever told God how much you love him and how thankful you are that he created you? If you haven't, or even if you have, take time now to thank God for the wonderful gift of life.

Play It

1. *Word Search*
Can you find the following Fruit of the Spirit in the puzzle below?

LOVE   GOODNESS
JOY   FAITHFULNESS
PEACE   GENTLENESS
PATIENCE   SELF-CONTROL
KINDNESS

```
X T W E G S E R C O P G
A Z I Y U U V K I V A E
V L O R T N O C F L E S
E J P U J L L S A D S S
M V T L S A O E I E S E
A N S S E O P L N T E A
I M S E S L A L B H N C
T P E A C E U T K J E P
H O N Z O F N E U A L V
E H D V H T L D N X T S
S I N T O L C A O P N A
S P I F C E P J J O E Y
A A K K X O L W E O G P
F N I P A T I E N C E C
G S N C L N N S O L D G
```

Pages 36–40

Learn It

1. God is always:
   a. changing
   b. angry
   c. the same
   d. confused

2. How is God's love different than human love?

   _____

   _____.

3. What is the key to true happiness?

   _____

   _____.

Think About It

1. How can you know God is trustworthy? How does knowing that God is trustworthy affect the way you think about prayer?

2. If you could ask God only three questions about himself, what would they be? Why?

3. What is your favorite thing about God that you learned in this section? What difference does knowing that thing make in your life?

Answers

Pages 12–15
Learn It

1. Any three of the following are correct:
   1) God loves balance 2) God cares about what he has created 3) God keeps things in order 4) God is trustworthy 5) No detail is too small for God 6) God is intelligent 7) God gave us rest.
2. 1) Intelligence 2) the God idea 3) conscience 4) beauty.
3. c) No one made God. God has always existed and will always exist.
4. The qualities of God that are not seen—his eternal power and the fact that he is God.

Pages 16–19
Learn It

1. The correct order is omnipotent, omnipresent, and omniscient.
2. One.
3. Because God made everything and nothing exists except what he has made.
4. 1) God the Father 2) God the Son 3) God the Holy Spirit. They are the same in that they are all one. They share the same nature. They are different in that they each have their own special jobs to do.

Do It

1. Electricity, radio waves, magnetism, wind, gravity.

Pages 20–23
Learn It

1. We both have spirits, we both have minds, we both have responsibilities, and we both have emotions.
2. God's relationship with his people was ruined by Adam and Eve's disobedience.
3. It means that we are all born sinful and separated from God.
4. Disobedience to God. There are many consequences of sin. For example, violence, famine, lies, greed, and so forth.

Play It

1. a) Father b) Abba c) The Word d) Wonderful Counselor e) Shepherd f) Rock of Israel g) King of Kings h) Lord of Lords i) Prince of Peace j) High Priest k) Alpha and Omega.

Pages 24–27
Learn It

1. They come from ourselves and the devil.
2. The correct order is c, e, a, b, d.

3. d) pure nothingness.
4. b) realize we are all Brahman.
5. a) only strict obedience to Islamic laws matters to God.

Pages 28–31
Learn It

1. God's single motivation is love. He can't do anything that is unloving because that would contradict his very nature. Asking God to do something unloving is like asking God not to be God, which is impossible, even for God.
2. Jesus. He shows God's love to us by: 1) caring about our pain 2) looking after our needs 3) helping us know the truth 4) welcoming us to himself 5) being kind.
3. Death. Jesus. He did this by dying on the cross.
4. The correct order is c, d, b, e, a.

Pages 32–35
Learn It

1. It is important to go to church to: 1) learn about God 2) grow together with others 3) help each other.
2. b) God's instruction manual; d) God's love letter.
3. d) He created us and he loves us as his children.
4. 1) We start to resemble Jesus 2) We become people others want to be with 3) We see God's fruit in our lives.

Play It

X	T	W	E	G	S	**E**	R	C	O	P	G
A	Z	I	**Y**	U	U	**V**	K	I	V	A	E
V	**L**	**O**	**R**	**T**	**N**	**O**	**C**	**F**	**L**	**E**	**S**
E	**J**	P	U	J	L	**L**	S	A	D	**S**	S
M	V	T	L	S	A	O	E	I	**E**	**S**	E
A	N	**S**	**S**	E	O	P	L	**N**	T	**E**	A
I	M	**S**	E	**S**	L	A	**L**	B	H	**N**	C
T	**P**	**E**	**A**	**C**	**E**	**U**	T	K	J	**E**	P
H	O	**N**	Z	O	**F**	N	E	U	A	**L**	V
E	H	**D**	V	H	T	L	**D**	N	X	**T**	S
S	I	**N**	T	O	L	C	A	**O**	P	**N**	A
S	P	**I**	F	C	E	P	J	J	**O**	**E**	Y
A	**A**	**K**	K	X	O	L	W	E	O	**G**	P
F	N	**I**	**P**	**A**	**T**	**I**	**E**	**N**	**C**	**E**	C
G	S	N	C	L	N	N	S	O	L	D	G

Pages 36–40
Learn It

1. c) the same.
2. God's love is infinite and unchanging. He will always love us no matter what. Human love can come and go depending on the circumstances or how we happen to feel.
3. The key to true happiness is a relationship with God.

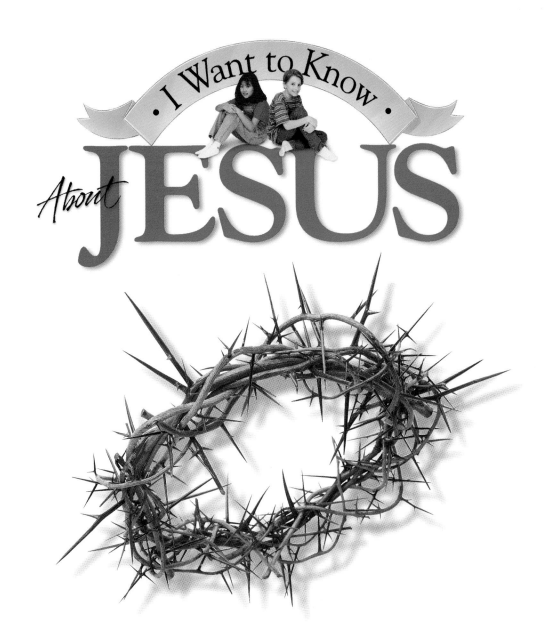

God Became a Man

Did you know Jesus has been alive with God forever?

Imagine an artist becoming part of his own painting! Impossible? God did something like this!

In the very beginning God, through his Son, an awesome artist called the Word, spoke and made the world. "In the beginning, the Word was already there. The Word was with God, and the Word was God. All things were made through him. Nothing that has been made was made without him" (John 1:1, 3). God, through the Word, made every living creature. Then he made people, Adam and Eve, to be like him and be his children. He gave them a beautiful garden to live in and rules to follow so they would have a great life. (A key rule was "Do not eat fruit from the Knowledge tree!") And he gave them free will so they could choose to obey him and be his children. Or not.

Everything should have been fine. But Satan, an important angel who became God's enemy, disguised himself as a snake. "You don't have to obey God's rules," he said. "Eat the Knowledge fruit. You'll become like God."

Unfortunately, Adam and Eve ate it up. They chose to listen to Satan,

and that wrecked everything!

God was very sad. He sent Adam and Eve away. He still loved them, but sin separates them from God, who is holy. And everyone who came after them (including us) was born sinful and separated from God, too. God had said, "If you sin, you'll die." So the penalty had to be paid.

Satan thought he'd won. But God had a plan! His plan would pay for everyone's sins so we could all be

Angels with a Promise

God chose human parents for his Son: Mary, and her fiancé, Joseph, from Nazareth. God sent the angel Gabriel to tell Mary, "God is very pleased with you. You will become pregnant and give birth to a son. You must name him Jesus. He will be great and will be called the Son of the Most High God" (Luke 1:30–32). Mary asked how this could happen since she wasn't married. Gabriel said, "The Holy Spirit will come to you. The power of the Most High God will cover you. So the holy one that is born will be called the Son of God" (Luke 1:35).

Joseph found out Mary was pregnant. He knew the baby wasn't his. God sent an angel to Joseph in a dream. He said, "Don't be afraid to take Mary home as your wife. The baby inside her is from the Holy Spirit. She is going to have a son. You must give him the name Jesus. That is because he will save his people from their sins" (Matthew 1:20–21).

So Joseph made Mary his wife.

with him again. God sent his Son, the Word, to die for us. God's Son, Jesus, could pay for our sins because he was holy and sinless. Jesus entered his own "painting" and became one of the people he'd created! "The Word became a human being. He made his home with us…. He came from the Father" (John 1:14). Jesus loved us. He was and is God, the Word. He became human and lived as one of us!

1) *In the beginning there was only God.*

2) *God created the world.*

3) *God made Adam and Eve.*

4) *Adam and Eve disobeyed God and sinned.*

God's Son Is a Baby

When it was almost time for Mary's baby to be born, the Roman ruler Caesar Augustus made a law that everyone had to go to their hometown to be counted. Joseph belonged to the family line of King David, so he and Mary had to travel from Nazareth up to Bethlehem, the town of David. It must have been a rough journey for Mary.

When they arrived, Bethlehem was so busy that the inn had no room, so Mary and Joseph stayed in a stable. While they were there, Mary gave birth to a baby boy. They called him Jesus, as the angel had said. They wrapped baby Jesus in cloths and made a bed for him in a manger.

That night in the hills near Bethlehem, something amazing happened! An angel of the Lord appeared to shepherds in a field. All around him shone a light. The shepherds were terrified!

The angel told them not to be afraid. He said, "I bring you good news of great joy…. Today in the town of David a Savior has been born to you. He is Christ the Lord. Here is how you will know I am telling you the truth. You will find a baby wrapped in strips of cloth and iying in a manger" (Luke 2:10–12).

The shepherds rushed into Bethlehem and found Mary, Joseph, and baby Jesus. He was wrapped in strips of cloth and lying in a manger just like the angel had said. The shepherds told everyone what had happened. All the people who heard about it were amazed.

God's Son, the Word, was born into our world as the baby Jesus.

Rome: The Villages That Ruled the World

About 700 years before Jesus was born, a group of villages in Italy joined together to become Rome. This new city was ruled by kings for 200 years. Then it was ruled by two consuls elected each year. One-hundred-fifty years later Rome ruled all of Italy and was conquering other lands with its armies. But the army generals started fighting amongst themselves.

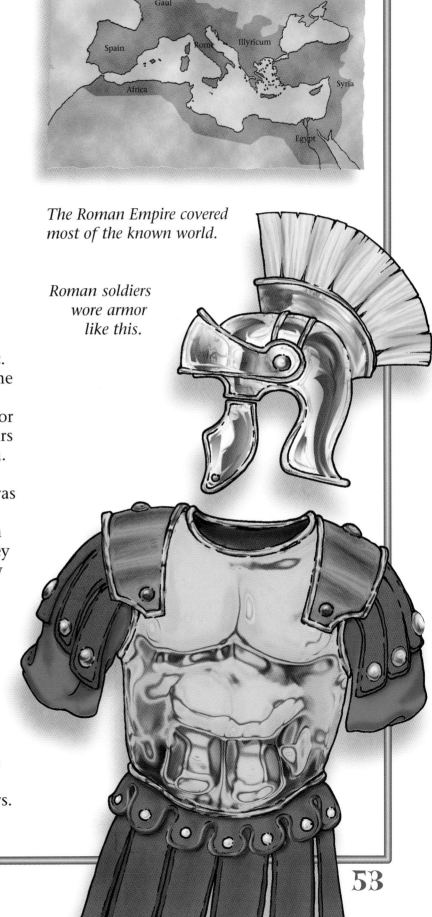

The Roman Empire covered most of the known world.

Roman soldiers wore armor like this.

Rulers and More Rulers

Julius Caesar was elected consul in 59 B.C. He defeated the other generals, unified the empire, and declared himself dictator for life. But the Romans didn't want a dictator and killed him. There were more civil wars until Julius's adopted son, Octavian, won. He restored peace and became Caesar Augustus, the first Roman emperor. He was ruling when Jesus was born.

Whenever the Romans conquered an area, they made the people pay taxes. They stationed very tough soldiers in these new provinces to make sure Roman laws were obeyed and taxes were paid. Their army built excellent roads between major cities and they made Greek the common language throughout the empire.

Rome appointed a man named Herod to be king of Judea where the Jews lived. He ruled over them until a few years after Jesus was born. He built Roman-style cities and tried to introduce Roman customs to the Jews. He built a beautiful temple in Jerusalem for the Jews. This is the temple Jesus visited.

Jesus Grows Up

Have you ever seen a shooting star or comet?

When Jesus was born, Wise Men east of Judea saw an unusual star. They believed it meant a special king had been born to the Jews, so they journeyed to the palace in Jerusalem to look for him. (Where else would a king be?) But the baby wasn't there.

King Herod was upset. He wanted to be the only king. He asked the Jewish leaders where the special King of the Jews would be born. They studied the Scriptures and said, "Bethlehem." The Wise Men found Jesus there with his mother.

They worshiped him and gave him expensive gifts.

That night God warned the Wise Men not to tell Herod about Jesus, so they went home a different way. In a dream, an angel told Joseph to escape to Egypt because Herod wanted to kill Jesus. Joseph got his family up and left right away. The angel was right. Herod killed many babies in Bethlehem hoping the "King of the Jews" would be one of them.

They stayed in Egypt until Herod died. Then, in another dream, an

Help Mary and Joseph find Jesus

angel told Joseph it was safe to go home. They returned to live in Nazareth.

Joseph, a carpenter, probably trained Jesus to work with him. They would have made furniture, tools, wheels, and utensils. Jesus likely started school when he was five and learned the Law, Genesis to Deuteronomy in the Bible, and how to read and write.

When Jesus was twelve, he went with his parents to the Passover feast in Jerusalem, to the beautiful temple Herod had built. After the feast, Mary and Joseph left for home. They realized that Jesus wasn't with them and then rushed back to Jerusalem to look for him. After three days, they found him in the temple, sitting with the teachers, listening and asking questions. The people were amazed at him!

Mary said, "Son, why have you treated us like this? Your father and I have been worried about you. We have been looking for you everywhere." "Why were you looking for me?" he asked. "Didn't you know I had to be in my Father's house?" (Luke 2:48–49). Mary and Joseph didn't understand that Jesus was talking about his real Father, God.

Jesus went back to Nazareth with his parents and obeyed them. "Jesus became wiser and stronger. He also became more and more pleasing to God and to people" (Luke 2:52).

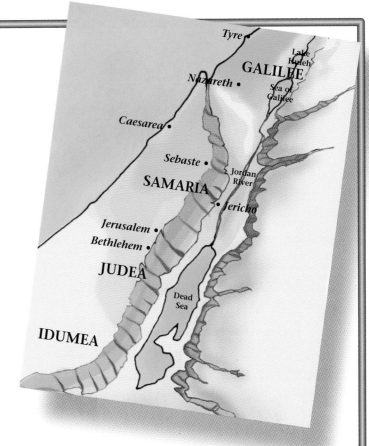

The Jewish World

Most Jews visited Herod's temple in Jerusalem once or twice a year. The rest of the time they went to the *synagogues* in their own villages to read from the Old Testament and pray.

The Jews had two main political/religious parties. The *Sadducees* were most of the rich. They tried to stay wealthy by cooperating with the Romans. The *Pharisees* were more popular among the common people. They talked about keeping all the rules and details of the Law. The *Sanhedrin* was a Jewish ruling counsel made up of these two groups. They were in charge of everyday life for the Jews.

Many of the Jews hated being ruled by the Romans. They remembered God's promise to send the *Messiah* to *save* the Jews from their enemies. They thought the Messiah would lead an army and defeat the Romans. Jesus didn't come to fight the Romans, so few people believed he was the one they were waiting for.

Baptized!

Jesus had a cousin named John who was a prophet living in the desert. His message was simple. "Repent [turn back to God] so your sins can be forgiven. The Kingdom of God is near!" When people repented, John baptized them in the Jordan River. Baptism was a symbol of being cleansed from sin.

One day John looked up and saw Jesus in the crowd! He pointed to Jesus and said, "Look! The Lamb of God! He takes away the sin of the world!" (John 1:29). Jesus asked John to baptize him. John protested. After all, Jesus didn't need to repent because he had never sinned! But Jesus said, "'Let it be this way for now. It is right for us to do this. It carries out God's holy plan.' Then John agreed. As soon as Jesus was baptized, he came up out of the water. At that moment heaven was opened. Jesus saw the Spirit of God coming down on him like a dove. A voice from heaven said, 'This is my Son, and I love him. I am very pleased with him'" (Matthew 3:15–17).

Later, Jesus told his followers to be baptized and to baptize others. That's one reason Christians get baptized today. It shows everyone that

God loves us and sent his Son to cleanse us from our sins.

Different churches baptize in different ways. The way it's done is not as important as the reason it's done and what it means: The water is a symbol of Jesus' blood washing away our sins. And baptism represents a commitment of the person's life to God.

Temptation Conquered!

Satan tricked the first people into disobeying God. Now he tried it with Jesus. He was trying to wreck God's plan. If Jesus gave in to temptation, he wouldn't be able to save the world like God had planned.

After Jesus' baptism, the Holy Spirit led him into the desert. After forty days without food, guess what? He got hungry. Satan told him to make bread out of the stones. He tried to convince Jesus that he deserved to have whatever he wanted. Jesus quoted from the Old Testament and refused.

Satan took Jesus to the top of the temple and told Jesus to jump. This time Satan tried quoting Scripture. He misquoted a psalm, telling Jesus he could do whatever he wanted, even jump off the temple, and nothing bad would happen! Again Jesus refused by quoting the Bible.

Finally, Satan took Jesus to a high mountain and showed him all the powerful kingdoms of the world. He told Jesus he'd give them to him if Jesus worshiped him. Jesus said, "Get away from me, Satan! It is written, 'Worship the Lord your God. He is the only one you should serve'" (Matthew 4:10).

Jesus Helps Us

We get tempted in similar ways. We want to do things our way instead of God's. Jesus understands what temptation is like. And he knows how we can conquer it. He knew that what God and the Bible said was the truth. So he trusted God and kept his focus on him instead of what he could get for himself. Temptation is Satan's trick to lead us away from the truth. We can fight temptation with the truth of the Bible. We can ask God for help, keep our focus on him, and trust him and Jesus to help us. They will. They love us!

Jesus knows and understands how we feel.

Disciple School

Imagine you're a young Jew in Jesus' time and want to study God's Word. You would look around your neighborhood at the rabbis (teachers). Then you would choose the rabbi you respected, the one you believed really knew the Scriptures.

You would join your *rabbi's* students and sit around him in a classroom. You would listen, ask questions, and memorize what he said until you knew the meaning of the various passages and laws.

However, *understanding* is only part of knowing God's Word. You'd also have to learn how to *live* according to the Torah. So you'd watch your teacher's life carefully. You and the other students or

disciples would become your rabbi's servants. When your teacher was out and about, you'd walk behind him. You would spend most of your time with him. You'd have a close relationship with him until he decided you were ready to be a teacher yourself. By then you would think, believe, and live like him.

This teaching method was common at that time. Jesus used this teaching method, too. His disciples followed him around, served him, lived with him wherever he went, listened carefully to his teachings, and asked questions. They had a close relationship with Jesus and tried to

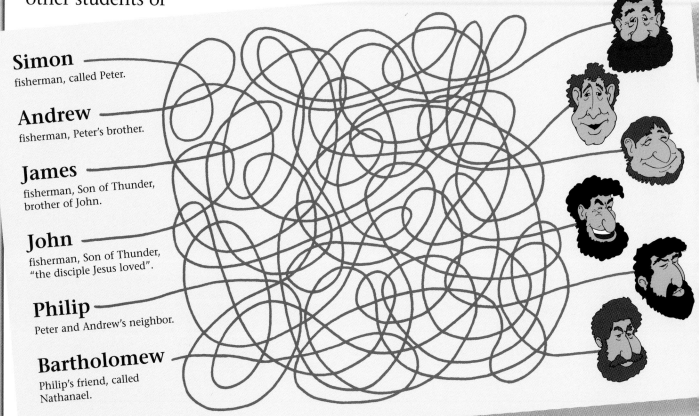

Simon
fisherman, called Peter.

Andrew
fisherman, Peter's brother.

James
fisherman, Son of Thunder,
brother of John.

John
fisherman, Son of Thunder,
"the disciple Jesus loved".

Philip
Peter and Andrew's neighbor.

Bartholomew
Philip's friend, called
Nathanael.

be like him. But Jesus' disciples didn't choose Jesus as their teacher. Jesus chose them! He chose twelve men. And his disciples didn't learn sitting in a classroom. Jesus taught in public places, on the seashore, in fields, and while they walked around the country.

Jesus chose ordinary men. They were mostly fishermen, but one was a tax collector and one was a "zealot" (someone willing to fight to be free from the Romans). They were people like you and me. Some of them had tempers (Jesus called two of them "Sons of Thunder" because of that), they doubted (remember "Doubting Thomas"?), sometimes they didn't understand, and later on they ran away when Jesus was arrested. But Jesus chose them. And he chooses us.

Girls Welcome

"No girls allowed!" Rabbis didn't teach women. But Jesus did! "The Twelve were with him. So were some women. . . . These women were helping to support Jesus and the Twelve with their own money" (Luke 8:1–3).

Some of these women were Mary Magdalene, Joanna, Mary, Salome the mother of the disciples James and John, and Susanna. Jesus had other women friends, like Mary and Martha, the sisters of Lazarus, the man he raised from the dead.

Women were the first to find out Jesus was no longer dead. Women were important to Jesus!

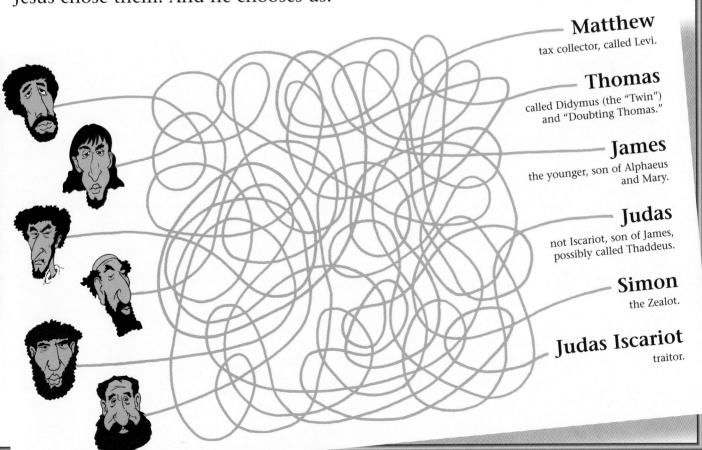

Matthew
tax collector, called Levi.

Thomas
called Didymus (the "Twin") and "Doubting Thomas."

James
the younger, son of Alphaeus and Mary.

Judas
not Iscariot, son of James, possibly called Thaddeus.

Simon
the Zealot.

Judas Iscariot
traitor.

Amazing Miracles

What's awesome and amazing? A miracle! Better yet, many miracles! Jesus' whole life was full of miracles, from before his birth to after his death and everywhere in between. Jesus experienced miracles and he performed miracles.

People Miracles

Jesus healed: lepers (people with a serious skin disease), at least five blind people, Peter's mother-in-law, a paralyzed man, a man with a withered hand, a woman who'd bled for twelve years, a deaf and mute man, a woman who'd been bent over for eighteen years, a man who couldn't talk, a man who'd been disabled for thirty-eight years, a man whose ear had been cut off, and, from a distance, one official's sick servant and another's sick son.

He drove out evil spirits from: "many," a boy, a man in the synagogue, and at least two violent, super-strong, chain-breaking, tomb-haunting men.

He raised from the dead: a twelve-year-old girl, a widow's only son, Lazarus (after he'd been dead four days).

He fed: 5000+ people with five loaves of bread and two fish, 4000+ people with seven loaves and a few small fish. The "+" is all the women and children—we don't know how many!

Nature Miracles

Jesus filled Peter's fishing nets so full they began to break, turned water into wine at a wedding, calmed a storm, walked on water, made a fig tree dry up, and told Peter to go fishing and in the first fish's mouth would be a coin to pay their taxes. After Jesus rose from the dead, he turned the disciples' no-fish night into a too-many-fish-for-the-net night.

Jesus raised the dead.

Jesus walked on water.

Jesus fed the hungry.

Jesus healed the sick.

The Meaning of Miracles

Jesus had a job to do while he was here as a man. A big part of his job was to show people what God was like. Doing miracles was a way to show people that God cared. Jesus showed people God loved them by doing miracles.

Jesus was God. He *told* people what God was like and he *showed* them, by his life and actions. He showed them God cared about little things as well as big ones. (His first miracle was to make water into wine just so his mother's friends wouldn't be embarrassed!)

By healing people, he showed us God is more powerful than sickness and death. He also showed us that God can take care of our needs and then some: Remember the feeding of the 5000+? There was oodles of food left over!

Some saw the miracles and didn't believe, but others did. For example, one night during a storm, the disciples were crossing the lake in their boat. Jesus walked on the water toward them. When he got into the boat, the wind died down. "Then those in the boat worshiped Jesus. They said, 'You really are the Son of God!'" (Matthew 14:33). They *knew* he was God because of the great miracle he had done!

Teaching with a Difference

Ever had a teacher you loved to listen to, who was interesting and made you think? We can tell from people's responses to Jesus that he was a great teacher. "The crowds were amazed at his teaching. He taught like one who had authority. He did not speak like their teachers of the law" (Matthew 7:28–29).

These people often heard rabbis and Pharisees teach. But Jesus amazed them! What made him different? He taught as if he "had authority." The rabbis taught what other people said. They didn't teach anything new.

Not Jesus! He'd say things like, "You've heard it said" and quote a famous saying. "Love your neighbor. Hate your enemy." Then he'd add, "But I say" and he'd say something new. "Love your enemies. Pray for those who hurt you" (Matthew 5:43–44). He had authority to add it because he was God.

Jesus also put a new emphasis on old things. He said it's not only important to do the right thing on the outside, we must change on the inside and act from hearts that are right.

The Pharisees believed that to be religious you had to follow all the rules. But Jesus taught that religion isn't about following the rules or obeying detailed commands. It's about a relationship with God.

That's why he taught his disciples how to pray so that they could talk to God whenever they wanted, thanking him, and telling him their needs. Prayer helped them get to know God better.

The Pharisees liked to show off how good and generous they were. But Jesus taught us to do good quietly, without expecting

Jesus walked everywhere, probably in sandals like these.

anything in return. He showed that a widow who gave only two pennies was more generous in her heart than a rich person who gave a big gift from great wealth.

Jesus' teaching was almost the opposite of the Pharisees' teaching. No wonder he got people's attention!

Jesus' New Teachings

Be Born Again:

"No one can see God's kingdom without being born again. No one can enter God's kingdom without being born through water and the Holy Spirit. People give birth to people. But the Spirit gives birth to spirit. God loved the world so much that he gave his one and only Son. Anyone who believes in him will not die but will have eternal life" (John 3:3, 5–6, 16).

The Lord's Prayer:

"This is how you should pray. 'Our Father in heaven, may your name be honored. May your kingdom come. May what you want to happen be done on earth as it is done in heaven. Give us today our daily bread. Forgive us our sins, just as we also have forgiven those who sin against us. Keep us from falling into sin when we are tempted. Save us from the evil one'" (Matthew 6:9–13).

Jesus, the Great Storyteller

"Once upon a time." These words mean a story is coming. Everyone likes stories! Jesus knew that, and told a lot of them. But many of his started with, "The kingdom of God is like." Then he'd launch into a story or parable that compared something people knew, like seeds or sheep, to things they didn't know, like God's kingdom. The comparisons helped them understand the kingdom. For example, Jesus spent time with people like tax collectors that the Jews looked down on and called "sinners." They thought God wanted them to avoid sinners. So Jesus told a story to help them understand that God wants to save sinners—"lost" people.

He said, "Suppose one of you has 100 sheep and loses one of them. Won't he leave the 99 in the open country? Won't he go and look for the one lost sheep until he finds it? When he finds it, he will joyfully put it on his shoulders and go home. Then he will call his friends and neighbors together. He will say, 'Be joyful with me. I have found my lost sheep.' I tell you, it will be the same in heaven. There will be great joy when one sinner turns away from sin. Yes, there will be more joy than for 99 godly people who do not need to turn away from their sins" (Luke 15:3–7).

His disciples asked why he used parables. He told them they had been given the chance to understand the secrets of God's kingdom. Jesus meant that those who wanted to understand his stories and teaching would. Those who didn't, would just hear a story.

Great Parables

The Prodigal Son Parable teaches that God is the best father we can imagine! A son left home and did wrong, foolish things. He spent everything he had and was starving. Finally, he decided to go home and ask for forgiveness. The father was so happy that he threw a party for him! Our Father, God, is like that (Luke 15:11–32).

The Good Samaritan Parable teaches that our neighbor is anyone in need. A Jewish man was beaten by robbers and left for dead. Jewish leaders walked by without helping. A Samaritan (Jews disliked Samaritans) stopped to help. Who acted like a good neighbor? (Luke 10:25–37)

The Sower and Seeds teaches us that people respond to Jesus in different ways. A farmer plants in different kinds of soil. Some seeds don't grow, some get choked by weeds, some have shallow roots and wither, and some grow and give a good crop (Matthew 13:1–23).

The Weeds Parable tells us we can't always tell who belongs to God's kingdom and who doesn't. An enemy sowed bad seed in a field. The owner said to let the weeds grow with the wheat. They'd sort it out at harvest. We shouldn't judge people. Instead, we should let God sort out who belongs to him (Matthew 13:24–30).

The Parable of the House Built on Rock teaches that when we live God's way things work out for the best. Jesus said people who heard his words and lived by them were wise like a house-builder who built on rock. But foolish people were like those who built on sand. A storm came and CRASH! No more sand-house (Matthew 7:24–27).

Jesus' Last Supper

Long ago, about 1500 years before Jesus, the Jews (Israelites) were slaves in Egypt. The Egyptian king, Pharaoh, was stubborn. He didn't want to set them free. God sent plagues to show the Egyptians he was more powerful than their so-called "gods." In the last plague, every firstborn child in the land would die.

Moses, the Israelite leader, told his people to kill a lamb and put some of its blood on the top and sides of their doors. God said he would see it and pass over (skip) any house with blood on the door. The lamb died in place of the eldest child. Meanwhile, the Israelites ate their lamb dinner with unleavened (flat) bread and wine. This was the first "Passover." That night the first-born children of all the Egyptians died, but the Israelite children were safe. Pharaoh let the Israelites go. Jews celebrate the Passover every year as a reminder of their escape.

Jesus celebrated the Passover with his disciples. This time it would be different!

After the meal, Jesus took the unleavened bread. "He gave thanks and broke it. He handed it to them and said, 'This is my body. It is given for you. Every time you eat it, do it in memory of me.'" After supper he took the wine. "'This cup is the new covenant [agreement] in my blood. . . . It is poured out to forgive the sins of many'" (Luke 22:19–20;

Matthew 26:28). Jesus was about to become the Passover lamb. He would die instead of everyone who had sinned.

The "Supper" Today

When Adam and Eve sinned God said the punishment was death. Later he made a covenant with the Israelites. They would regularly bring sacrifices to pay for their sins. Animals would die in their place, and God would forgive them.

Now, in Jesus, God was about to make a new covenant with all people. In this new agreement, there's no need for regular sacrifices. Only one is needed. God would provide it himself: his sinless Son, Jesus. When Jesus told the disciples to eat the bread and drink the cup, he was telling them to accept what he was about to do for them.

Jesus' last supper with his disciples started a new tradition that we still celebrate almost 2000 years later! People have

different names for it, but when we eat the bread and drink from the cup, we're all saying, "I accept what Jesus did for me. I know he paid for my sins so that I wouldn't have to die. Thank you!"

Jesus' Enemies

Jesus preached the truth, told people about God's kingdom, and showed them God's love. But he still had enemies. The Pharisees, Sadducees, chief priests, and scribes all hated Jesus. They loved to be respected and to have power and authority. They were afraid Jesus would change that.

The Pharisees liked to impress people. They felt it was their job to keep all Jews obeying the Law. They made lots of new laws. They were sure they were God's favorites!

Along came Jesus telling everyone the Pharisees weren't as wonderful as they thought: The Pharisees had it wrong. God wanted people to obey him from love, not fear; to treat people with kindness, not to be proud and judgmental. The Sanhedrin with its Pharisees, Sadducees, and priests, knew that if people listened to Jesus instead of them, they'd lose their power. Or the Romans might get upset and take their power away.

They decided it was time to do something about Jesus! Since only the Romans could put people to death, the Jews had to convince Pilate, the Roman governor, that Jesus was against Caesar and deserved to die.

They knew that if they arrested Jesus when he was surrounded by the people there would be a riot. If only they could get him alone.

Judas Paid Off

"Traitor." "Tattle-tale." "Judas." We all know these words. But why do we use "Judas" to mean someone who betrays a friend? Because of Judas Iscariot, Jesus' disciple.

Judas snuck off to see the Pharisees. "Hey!" he said. "You want Jesus? I can give you Jesus. But it'll cost you." So the Pharisees gave Judas thirty pieces of silver (about five months' pay)

to tell them where they could quietly capture Jesus.

Jesus and the disciples were in the Garden of Gethsemane. Peter told Jesus, "I will give my life for you." Jesus answered, "Will you really? . . . Before the rooster crows, you will say three times that you don't know me!" (John 13:37, 38) Later, the disciples slept while Jesus prayed, "My Father, if it is possible, take this cup of suffering away from me. But let what you want be done, not what I want" (Matthew 26:39).

The Garden of Gethsemane where Jesus prayed.

Betrayed!

Suddenly soldiers, officials, and a crowd with swords and clubs (sent from the Jewish leaders) arrived in the quiet Garden. Judas was leading them! He betrayed Jesus. When Jesus was arrested, the disciples ran away.

Jesus was taken to the high priest's house. The Sanhedrin was there even though they weren't supposed to meet at night. They took him to Pilate, the Roman governor, saying that Jesus called himself "King of the Jews" and was against Caesar.

Peter had followed the crowd into the courtyard. Someone asked if he was Jesus' disciple. He said, "No!" This happened twice more. The third time Peter was so scared he swore and said, "I don't know this man you're talking about!" (Mark 14:71). Right away the rooster crowed. Peter remembered what Jesus had said. He ran out, crying.

Jesus was passed from the Jews to Pilate, to Herod, and back to Pilate. Pilate found Jesus innocent but, trying to please the Jews, had him beaten anyway. The Jews told Pilate he wasn't Caesar's friend if he let Jesus go. Pilate got scared and agreed to crucify Jesus.

Coins from Jesus' time.

Condemned to Death

Crucifixion was a horrible way to die. Roman solders were known for their cruelty. Jesus had already been beaten, mocked, spit on, whipped, and had a "crown" made of thorns pushed onto his head. Now he had to carry part of his own cross outside the city to the place called "Skull," "Golgotha," or "Calvary."

Jesus' hands and feet were nailed to the cross. Two robbers were crucified with him, one on each side. On the top of Jesus' cross Pilate put a sign: "This is the King of the Jews." One of the robbers believed this. He asked Jesus to remember him when he came into his kingdom. Jesus answered, "Today you will be with me in paradise" (Luke 23:43). Speaking about those who had put him on the cross, Jesus said, "Father, forgive them. They don't know what they are doing" (Luke 23:34).

Many strange things happened. At noon "the whole land was covered with darkness until three o'clock. The sun had stopped shining. Jesus cried out, 'My God, my God, why have you deserted me?' The temple curtain was torn in two. The earth shook. Tombs broke open. The bodies of many who had died were raised to life. Jesus called out in a loud voice, 'Father, into your hands I commit my very life.' After he said this, he took his last breath. He said, 'It is finished.' Then he bowed his head and died. The Roman commander and those guarding Jesus saw the earthquake and all that had happened. They were terrified. They exclaimed, 'He was surely the Son of God!'" (Matthew 27:45–46, 51–52, 54; Luke 23:44–46; John 19:30).

Satan used people to kill Jesus. He thought he'd won. He didn't know it was all part of God's plan. Friends of Jesus took his body down, wrapped it in burial cloths with some spices, and laid it in a tomb nearby.

Jesus had said he would rise again after three days. His enemies remembered. They asked Pilate to station Roman soldiers in front of Jesus' tomb in case his disciples tried to steal his body and pretend he'd risen from the dead.

Why Jesus Had to Die

God's plan was almost complete! Since Adam and Eve had sinned, God had been working to make a way for us to have the close relationship with him he'd wanted from the beginning. Sin separated us from God. The only way we could be forgiven once and for all was if someone sinless chose to pay for our sins and die in our place. Only God was sinless. So God chose to die for us.

God's Son, Jesus Christ, the Word who had made everything, became flesh like us and lived a perfect, sinless life. Then Jesus fulfilled God's plan and died a horrible death.

He died at Passover. He was the Passover lamb, the one who died instead of us, just like the lamb in the first Passover died in place of the first-born child. Now Jesus' blood paid for our sins. The Bible says, "Without the spilling of blood, no one can be forgiven" (Hebrews 9:22). And "Because of what the Son has done, we have been set free. Because of him, all of our sins have been forgiven" (Colossians 1:14).

What a plan! What love!

The Grave Is Empty!

The Roman soldiers stood guard over Jesus' tomb from Friday evening to Sunday morning. YAWN! Suddenly the earth shook. An angel rolled the stone away from the tomb! The Romans "were so afraid of him that they shook and became like dead men" (Matthew 28:4).

Some of Jesus' women followers came to the tomb. The angel said, "Don't be afraid. I know that you are looking for Jesus, who was crucified. He is not here! He has risen, just as he said he would! Come and see the place where he was lying. Go quickly! Tell his disciples, 'He has risen from the dead'" (Matthew 28:5–7). They ran to tell the news!

Peter and John ran to the tomb and found it empty. Later, the disciples were in a room and Jesus appeared! He spoke to them and ate with them. Jesus appeared many times over the next forty days and explained the Scriptures.

After forty days, Jesus led his disciples to the Mount of Olives. "Then he lifted up his hands and blessed them. While he was blessing them, he left them. He was taken up into heaven. They watched until a cloud hid him from their sight. . . . They kept on looking at the sky. Suddenly two men dressed in white clothing stood beside them. 'Men of Galilee,' they said, 'why do you stand here looking at the sky? Jesus has been taken away from you into heaven. But he will come back in the same way you saw him go'" (Luke 24:50–51; Acts 1:9–11).

Only God could have done that!

The huge stone was rolled away from Jesus' tomb.

Risen for Sure!

Was the resurrection real? Put these facts together.

- The Romans said Jesus was dead. People do not recover from crucifixion.

- Jesus was buried in a cave with one exit.

- His body was wrapped in cloths and spices. The myrrh used made the grave-clothes stick to the body so they'd be difficult to remove.

- A large stone (probably almost two tons) was rolled across the entrance.

- Roman soldiers guarded the tomb. Falling asleep on the job meant death for them!

A couple of days later:

- The tomb was empty.

- The huge stone had been moved away from the tomb, not just rolled uphill!

- The Roman guards were bribed to say the disciples stole the body while they slept. But neither they nor the disciples were punished for breaking Roman law.

- The grave-clothes were empty, as if his body had passed right through them.

- More than 500 people said Jesus appeared to them alive!

- The disciples changed from timid people hiding from the authorities, to bold people who suffered beatings and death because they believed Jesus rose from the dead.

The only story that fits the facts is that Jesus really did rise from the dead, just as Scripture and Jesus predicted!

Adapted from Josh McDowell's book Reasons Skeptics Should Consider Christianity.

Jesus in the World Today

Look for Israel on a world map. It's a tiny place by the Mediterranean Sea. What could such a small place have to offer the world? Only the greatest man who ever lived!

In some ways, Jesus' life doesn't seem unusual. (Let's ignore the miracles for a bit.) He was born in a tiny village. After his trip to Egypt, he never traveled more than 150 miles from home and all of that on foot. He was a carpenter until he was about thirty. Then he was a traveling preacher for three years with no home, very little money, and only the clothes on his back. He hung out with people others looked down on.

Then people turned against him, his friends ran away, and one of them betrayed him. He was condemned to death and nailed to a cross. As he died Roman soldiers gambled over his clothes. His body was put in a borrowed grave.

Jesus lived and died in obedience to God. And then something incredible happened. Jesus rose from the dead and changed things forever! In the almost 2000 years since then, this man from a tiny corner of the world has had a greater impact than anyone else who ever lived!

Jesus' followers wrote books and letters about his life and teachings that are among the most-read books in the world. Whole libraries have been written about Jesus and his teachings. Easter and Christmas are celebrated. Jesus' followers around the world number in the millions. His churches are in every major city, and in towns and villages throughout the world. Jesus' story has been translated into hundreds of languages so people everywhere can know him. Colleges, universities, and even nations have been started based on his teachings.

Jesus' life changed the world forever! That was God's plan.

Changed Lives

Have you ever tried to break a habit, like biting your fingernails? Changing is hard! Just think, then, how hard it is to change from a frightened person into a brave one! That's what happened to Jesus' disciples almost overnight! How? Because Jesus rose from the dead. That showed the disciples he really was the Messiah they'd been looking for. It gave them courage to stand up for the truth.

After Jesus died, the disciples hid in the upper room with the door locked. They were afraid the Jews would kill them next. That's where Jesus found them and showed them he was alive again. When he rose to heaven he promised them that a friend, a Comforter, would help them. When the Comforter, the Holy Spirit, came, they changed completely (see Acts 2). Instead of hiding, they boldly told people about Jesus. They were threatened, arrested, and beaten, but they didn't stop! They were no longer afraid of people who could only kill their bodies. If Jesus rose from the dead, they would too. Their changed lives showed they knew Jesus was alive. (Would you die for something you knew was a lie?)

Jesus has been changing lives ever since. And he can change your life too. Just ask him. It's as easy as that!

Jesus and Me

Q **Why does Jesus want us to follow him?**

A Jesus told the people to follow him because he is the way to God, heaven, and eternal life. When Jesus was on earth, the disciples and others followed him by walking close

to him and listening to his words. Today, we follow Jesus by copying his example and by doing what he says. We can find out what he says by reading the Bible.

Key Verses: "Then Jesus spoke to his disciples. He said, 'If anyone wants to follow me, he must say no to himself. He must pick up his cross and follow me. If he wants to save his life, he will lose it. But if he loses his life for me, he will find it. What good is it if someone gains the whole world but loses his soul? Or what can anyone trade for his soul?'" (Matthew 16:24–26)

Q **How do you get Jesus in your heart?**

A You become a Christian by asking Jesus to take over your life. You know that you have done wrong things, that you have sinned, and you recognize that you need Jesus to forgive

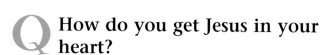

your sins. So you tell Jesus about your sins and that you are sorry, and you ask for his forgiveness. Then you do what Jesus says.

Key Verses: "But now God has shown us how to become right with him. The Law and the Prophets give witness to this. It has nothing to do with obeying the law. We are made right with God by putting our faith in Jesus Christ. That happens to all who believe. It is no different for the Jews than for anyone else. Everyone has sinned. No one measures up to God's glory. The free gift of God's grace makes all of us right with him. Christ Jesus paid the price to set us free" (Romans 3:21–24).

Q How can Jesus fit in my heart?

A When we say "heart," we mean deep down inside us where we really feel and believe. So when someone says, "Jesus lives in my heart," the person means that he has asked Jesus to be his Savior to forgive and take care of him

and that Jesus is in charge of his life. When someone asks Jesus to take over, God really does come inside. The Holy Spirit comes and lives inside that person. And the Holy Spirit can be in all of the people who love God at the same time. Jesus wants to be very close to you, too, like a good friend. Through the Holy Spirit, he wants to "live in your heart."

Key Verses: "That word contains the mystery that has been hidden for many ages. But now it has been made known to God's people. God has chosen to make known to them the glorious riches of that mystery. He has made it known among those who aren't Jews. And here is what it is. Christ is in you. He is your hope of glory" (Colossians 1:26–27).

Q When is Jesus coming back?

A Before Jesus left the earth many years ago, he promised to return some day. And after Jesus went up into the clouds, angels said he would come back eventually. No one knows exactly when that will happen. It could be any day now. For Christians, this is a wonderful event to look forward to. Christ's return will be the beginning of the end for Satan and all evil in the world. Won't it be great to see Jesus in person! Although no one knows when Christ will return, he told us to be ready. This means living the way he would want us to, using our time wisely, and telling others about God's Good News.

Key Verses: "[Jesus is speaking] No one knows about that day or hour. Not even the angels in heaven know. The Son does not know. Only the Father knows. . . . So keep watch. You do not know on what day your Lord will come" (Matthew 24:36, 42).

Adapted from *101 Questions Children Ask About God*, Tyndale House Publishers, 1992. Used by permission.

The Plan Is a Success!

God's plan worked! Ever since Adam and Eve sinned, God was working to make a way for people (that's us) to have the kind of relationship with him he wanted. He knew we would only really be happy if we were close to him. But sin made a wall between us. God needed someone to break down the wall. He needed a perfect person, someone without sin, who would be willing to die to pay for our sin.

So God got everything ready and made sure the timing was perfect. Then he sent his Son the Word, through whom he created everything, to be born as a baby and live as a human. He called him "Jesus," which means "Savior."

Jesus grew up as an ordinary person. He lived a perfect, obedient life. He never sinned. Like us, he faced temptations and had struggles. He grew and learned. The Bible tells us "Jesus was God's Son. But by suffering he learned what it means to obey" (Hebrews 5:8). He died for us, to pay for our sins. And he broke down the wall sin had made between us and God. God accepted Jesus' death in place of ours and forgave us our sins!

That was God's plan. That's why Jesus came: to show us what God was like, to teach us how to relate to God, and to pay for our sins so that we could be together with God as God had planned even before he made us.

All we have to do is accept what Jesus did, ask for forgiveness, and, with God's help, try to live the way he wants us to.

Then we wait for Jesus to come back and take us to heaven with him. That's where we'll be with God fully and be completely happy!

Questions and Activities

Pages 50–53

Learn It

1. How long has Jesus been alive?
   a. 2000 years
   b. 1,000,000 years
   c. forever
   d. since 1917

2. What was God's plan to deal with sin?

   _____

   _____.

3. Why was Jesus able to pay for our sin?

   _____

   _____.

4. Which of the following statements about Jesus is true?
   a. Jesus is God
   b. Jesus is a god
   c. Jesus is a man
   d. Jesus is an angel
   e. all of the above are true
   f. only "a" and "c" are true

5. How did Mary become pregnant with Jesus?

   _____

   _____.

   Why do you suppose God did this?

   _____

   _____.

   Why wasn't Jesus simply born through Joseph?

   _____

   _____.

6. What empire ruled Israel during Jesus' time?

   _____.

7. What was the name of the king of Judea when Jesus was born?

   _____.

8. What was the common language of the Roman Empire?

   _____.

Think About It

1. Why do you think God chose to come to earth as a baby?

2. Jesus had to grow up from a baby to a man, just like we do. How do you think his life was like yours? How was it different?

Pages 54–57

Learn It

1. Why did Herod want to kill Jesus?

   _____

   _____.

2. Match the following names with their definitions below:

   _____ synagogue

   _____ Sanhedrin

   _____ Sadducees

   _____ Pharisees

   _____ Messiah

   a. The political/religious party that cooperated with the Romans

b. The political/religious party who kept the details of the law
c. The place where people went to read the Old Testament and pray
d. The Jewish ruling council
e. The name of the person whom the Jews hoped would save them from their enemies

3. Why didn't John want to baptize Jesus?
a. John was out of water
b. Jesus was too tall
c. The lineup was too long and John was already tired
d. John thought he was unworthy even to untie Jesus' sandals, never mind baptize him

4. What happened when Jesus was baptized?

_____

_____.

5. Why should Christians get baptized today?

_____

_____.

6. Why did Satan tempt Jesus?

_____

_____.

7. What did Jesus use to resist Satan's temptations?

_____

_____.

Think About It

1. Is it wrong to be tempted? Why or why not?

2. How does knowing that Jesus was tempted in every way that we are (Hebrews 4:15) help you deal with temptation? How can you fight temptation?

3. There are a number of elements in the story of Jesus as a child in the temple that you can relate to your own experiences. Read the story in Luke 2:41–52 and answer the following discussion questions.

How do you think Jesus' parents felt when they found out he wasn't with them?

Have you ever been lost? How did it feel?

What was Jesus doing when his parents found him in the temple?

What did the teachers and other people at the temple think of Jesus?

Do you think Jesus was too young to be asking about God? Why or why not?

Have you ever felt or been told that you're too young to be asking about God? How did you respond? Do you think we're ever too young for God? Too old? Why or why not?

Why did Jesus tell his mother that he was in his Father's house? It doesn't seem that Jesus' parents understood him at this point. Can you think of a time when you thought your parents didn't understand you? How did that feel?

Think about a time when you were doing something fun and your parents asked you to come home with them. How did you feel? Did you obey them? Why or why not?

Why do you think Jesus became wiser and more pleasing to God and to people?

How can you become wiser and more pleasing to God and people?

Pages 58–61

Learn It

1. What was the name for a religious teacher in Jesus' time?

_____.

What were a religious teacher's students called?

_____.

2. What kind of men did Jesus choose as his disciples?
   a. intellectuals
   b. dunces
   c. good looking people
   d. ordinary men

3. What are two ways in which Jesus was different from other rabbis of his day?

   _____,

   _____.

4. What are the names of three women who were close to Jesus?

   _____,

   _____,

   _____.

5. Why did Jesus perform miracles?

   _____

   _____.

Think About It

1. Would you have wanted to be one of Jesus' disciples? Why or why not? What do you think would have been the best part about being Jesus' disciple? The worst?

2. Why do you think girls were important to Jesus?

3. What do Jesus' miracles mean to you? How do they change the way you look at the world? How do they affect the way you pray?

4. Why do you think some people didn't believe that Jesus was God, even after seeing him perform miracles?

5. Do you think Jesus can still do miracles today? Why or why not? Have you ever heard of a miracle happening during modern times? Describe what happened. Did you find it difficult to believe? Why or why not? What finally made you believe it (or not believe it)?

Play It

1. Jesus used the Scriptures to overcome Satan's temptations in the desert. The Bible is full of all sorts of practical advice and instructions from God to help us deal with every situation in life. See if you can be like Jesus and use God's Word to help you overcome the following temptations.

   Your friend wants to tell you an inappropriate story during recess. What would Jesus do? (Read Philippians 4:8.)

   You get to your car after buying a new basketball and realize the clerk gave you too much change. What would Jesus do? (Read Mark 10:19.)

   Your parents tell you to get your chores done after school before you go out and play, but they won't be home for an hour. What would Jesus do? (Read Matthew 19:19.)

   You've just finished building a beautiful sand castle on the beach when a girl runs by and stomps all over it. You notice she has a beautiful sand castle of her own just a few feet away. What would Jesus do? (Read Luke 6:29.)

   Everyone is saying bad things about a boy at school. He did do something wrong, and he's really sorry about it. But now none of your friends will talk to him or hang out with him. What would Jesus do? (Read Matthew 7:3–5.)

Pages 62–65

Learn It

1. What made Jesus' teaching different from that of the Pharisees and other rabbis?

   _____

   _____.

   Why did Jesus have this authority?

   _____

   _____.

2. What are three ways in which Jesus' teaching was the opposite of the teaching of the Pharisees?

   _____,

   _____,

   _____.

3. How many times did Jesus say we must be born before we can see God's kingdom?

   _____.

4. Why did Jesus tell so many stories?

   _____

   _____.

5. Who did Jesus say creates more joy in heaven: one sinner who turns away from sin or 99 godly people who don't need to turn away from their sins?

   _____

   _____.

   Why do you think this is?

   _____

   _____.

6. Read the following parables in your Bible then match them with the lessons they teach below:

   _____ The Prodigal Son
   (Luke 15:11–32)

   _____ The Good Samaritan
   (Luke 10:25–37)

   _____ Weeds and the Wheat
   (Matthew 13:24–30)

   _____ Sower and the Seeds
   (Matthew 13:1–23)

   _____ The House on the Rock
   (Matthew 7:24–27)

   a. We shouldn't judge people. We should leave the judging up to God.
   b. When we live God's way, things work out for the best.
   c. God is our loving Father who loves us no matter who we are or what we've done.
   d. People respond to Jesus in different ways.
   e. Our neighbor is anyone who is in need.

Think About It

1. How does knowing that Christianity is about a relationship with God rather than following rules affect the way you think about being a Christian?

2. Which one of Jesus' parables is your favorite? Why is it important to you?

Do It

1. Choose one of the parables from pages 64–65 and rewrite the story in a modern setting. For example, you could rewrite the parable of the Good Samaritan. Jesus made a Samaritan the hero of this parable because in his

time Samaritans were despised by other people because they were half-Jewish and half-Canaanite. Nobody liked them. Jesus wanted to show his listeners that we shouldn't judge people on their race, appearance, or position in life. Now, ask yourself who are the Samaritans, that is, people who are despised, in today's society? Use this sort of person as your Samaritan.

Jesus made a priest and a Levite the "bad guys" in this parable because even though they were supposed to be good and go out of their way to help others they were often corrupt and too proud to get their hands dirty. Now, who are the people in today's society who think they have it all together and are too good for others? Use these sorts of people as the characters who pass by the wounded man.

Now you're all set to write your parable. Have fun with it. And don't just stop with one. Try rewriting a few of Jesus' parables. You can show them to your parents, your Sunday school teacher, or your friends—and ask them to help you act your new parables out.

Pages 66–69

Learn It

1. What event did the Passover celebrate?
   a. when God "passed over" the houses of the Israelites so their first-born children wouldn't be killed
   b. when the Israelite soccer team "passed over" the middle and scored the winning goal in the 564 B.C. World Cup
   c. when Saul was "passed over" as the king of Israel
   d. when the past was over

2. Why did Jesus ask his disciples to eat the bread and drink the wine at his last supper with them?

   _____

   _____.

   What did these elements represent?

   _____

   _____.

3. Why do we still celebrate the Last Supper today?

   _____

   _____.

4. What four groups of people were Jesus' enemies?

   _____,

   _____,

   _____,

   _____.

   Why did these people hate Jesus?

   _____

   _____.

5. How much was Judas paid to betray Jesus?

   _____.

6. How many times did Peter deny Jesus?

   _____.

   Why do you think he did it?

   _____

   _____.

7. Why did Pilate agree to crucify Jesus even though he knew Jesus was innocent?

_____

_____.

Think About It

1. Have you ever celebrated the Last Supper? If so, what does it mean to you? If you haven't celebrated it, talk to someone you know who has. What does it mean to them?

2. Think of a time when you were like Peter or Pilate and afraid to do what you knew was right. What happened? Why were you afraid? Were you able to overcome your fear? Why or why not? How do you think you can overcome your fear the next time you are in that sort of situation?

Pages 70–73

Learn It

1. What are three names for the place where Jesus was crucified?

_____,

_____,

_____.

2. Which of the following things *did not* happen when Jesus was crucified?
   a. people were brought back to life
   b. the stock market crashed
   c. an earthquake
   d. the sky grew dark
   e. all of the above

3. How many days did Jesus say it would take before he rose from the dead?

_____.

4. Who rolled the stone away from Jesus' tomb?

_____.

5. Who were the first people to find out that Jesus was alive?

_____.

6. When Jesus was lifted up into the sky, what did the voice from heaven tell the disciples?
   a. that Jesus was a defective robot who was being recalled for repairs
   b. that Jesus would return for them one day in his spaceship
   c. that Jesus would return one day the same way they saw him go
   d. that they had 10 seconds to get off the hill or they would be struck by lightning

7. List five reasons why we can know Jesus' resurrection was real:

_____,

_____,

_____,

_____,

_____.

Think About It

1. Jesus could have come down off the cross if he had wanted to—he can do anything—but he didn't. Why do you think he stayed there?

2. What was Jesus' attitude toward those who tortured and crucified Him? Have you ever felt like people were picking on you even though you were innocent? How did you react? What can you learn from Jesus' example about how to respond to people who are mean to you?

3. Why do you think Judas betrayed Jesus? What could make you betray a friend? Why is it wrong to betray people?

4. Imagine you are one of the disciples: you'd seen Jesus die, and now you hear he is alive again. How do you feel? Do you have a difficult time believing it? Why or why not?

5. To make things even more real for you, imagine you'd seen one of your friends die and then later heard that he or she was alive. Would you believe it? Why or why not? What would it take for you to believe it?

Pages 74–78

Learn It

1. What was Jesus' occupation until he was about 30 years old?
   a. roofer
   b. sanitary engineer
   c. musician
   d. carpenter

2. How long has it been since Jesus walked the earth as a man?
   a. approximately 2000 years
   b. exactly two weeks
   c. just over two centuries
   d. nearly two decades

3. Why did Jesus' disciples hide in the upper room after Jesus died?

   _____

   _____.

Think About It

1. What was the best thing you learned about Jesus in this section? Why? How has it changed the way you think about being a Christian?

Do It

1. Jesus lived so long ago and in a country so far away that sometimes it seems like the stories about him are just imaginary and they happened in an imaginary place. Nothing could be further from the truth! The Bible records real people and real events that happened in real places. To prove it to yourself, get a globe, an atlas, or a map of the world and find the following places where Jesus lived and ministered: Israel, Jerusalem, Bethlehem, the Sea of Galilee, Jericho, Nazareth.

2. *Before and After.* The disciples became changed people after Jesus rose from the dead. Has Jesus changed your life? If so, draw a picture of yourself before you met Jesus. What did you feel like? What did you look like? Then draw a picture of yourself after you met Jesus. What changed? How was your life better? More difficult? Once you've completed your picture, stick it up on your wall or keep it in your Bible as a constant reminder that since you met Jesus you are a new creation (2 Corinthians 5:17): the old has gone away, the new has come.

   If you haven't met Jesus yet, do you want to? All you have to do is invite him into your life. A good way to do it is through the following prayer. You can either pray it on your own or get your mom, dad, or pastor to help you.

   "Dear God, I know I'm a sinner. I've made wrong choices and done bad things.

   "I'm sorry. Please forgive me. I know your Son, Jesus, died for my sins, and I believe you raised him from the dead. I want Jesus as my Lord and Savior. Thank you for loving me and making me your child. Now, please fill me with your Holy Spirit, so I'll have the strength I need to obey you. In Jesus' name, Amen."

Answers

Pages 50–53
Learn It
1. c) forever.
2. Sending Jesus to die on the cross for us.
3. Because he is God and he is the perfect, sinless sacrifice.
4. f) Only "a" and "c" are true
5. Mary became pregnant through the Holy Spirit.
6. The Roman Empire.
7. Herod.
8. Greek.

Pages 54–57
Learn It
1. Because he wanted to be the only king in Judea.
2. The correct order is: c, d, a, b, e.
3. d) John thought he was unworthy even to untie Jesus' sandals, never mind baptize him.
4. Heaven was opened, the Spirit of God came down like a dove, and God said he was pleased with Jesus, his son.
5. To identify with Jesus.
6. He was trying to wreck God's plan.
7. Scripture.

Pages 58–61
Learn It
1. Rabbi; disciples.
2. d) ordinary men.
3. 1) He taught with authority 2) he chose his own disciples instead of waiting for his disciples to come to him.
4. Any three of the following are correct:
   1) Mary Magdalene 2) Joanna 3) Mary
   4) Salome the mother of James and John
   5) Susanna.
5. To show people what God is like and to show that he cares about everything in life, both big and small.

Play It
1. a) Don't listen to the story b) Return the change c) Do your chores before you play d) Forgive her and don't retaliate e) Swallow your pride and go befriend the boy.

Pages 62–65
Learn It
1. He taught with authority. Jesus had this authority because he was God.

2. 1) He taught new things instead of just restating old teachings. 2) He taught that religion isn't about rules, it's about a relationship with God. 3) He didn't show off and he taught people to do good things in secret.
3. Twice.
4. To help people understand the secrets of God's kingdom.
5. One sinner who turns away from sin.
6. The correct order is: c, e, a, d, b.

Pages 66–69
Learn It
1. a) when God "passed over" the houses of the Israelites so their first-born children wouldn't be killed.
2. To remember him. Wine represents his blood; bread represents his body.
3. To remember what Jesus did for us on the cross.
4. 1) Pharisees 2) Sadducees 3) chief priests 4) scribes. They hated Jesus because they loved to have power and authority and they were afraid Jesus would change all of that.
5. 30 pieces of silver.
6. Peter denied Jesus three times because he was afraid.
7. He was afraid that it would be reported back to Rome that he was no friend of Caesar's because he allowed Jesus to call himself a king. Caesar wanted to be the only king.

Pages 70–73
Learn It
1. 1) Golgotha 2) The Skull 3) Calvary.
2. b) the stock market crashed.
3. Three.
4. An angel.
5. Mary Magdalene and the other Mary.
6. c) that Jesus would return one day the same way they saw him go.
7. See page 71 for these answers.

Pages 74–78
Learn It
1. d) Carpenter.
2. a) Approximately 2000 years.
3. Because they were afraid the Jews would kill them next.

What Is the Bible?

Did you know God has a book out? His book is the most well-known, unique book ever written. It's the Bible! Why did God put this best-seller together? Here are four reasons:

His Autobiography

The Bible tells us about God's character and values, who he is and what he does, so we can begin to understand him.

His Plan

God wanted to tell us his plan for the world. You see, Adam and Eve disobeyed him and wrecked their relationship with God—and everyone else's relationship with God as well. But God had a plan to repair the relationship. The Bible tells us the story of God's plan and how he dealt with people.

A Love Letter

The Bible tells us *how* we can have a relationship with God. We all sin. You've probably noticed that. No one is perfect. God tells us how he dealt with sin and made a way for us to be together.

An Instruction Manual

God made the world to work in a certain way—a way that lines up with what he's like. It works by particular principles and rules—kind of like a computer works by certain commands and programs. The way to have the best life is to follow those rules

and principles. God wrote them down for us in the Bible so we'd know how to have a great life.

Notice that all the reasons he made the Bible are for US! The Bible is all about God and us. God gave us his book for *our sakes*: for *your* sake, so you can have a wonderful life and a great relationship with him.

It makes you want to know more, doesn't it? Keep reading!

Life's Instruction Manual

Everyone wants to be happy and have a fantastic life, but how? Well, if you want to know how to operate a VCR or put together a model car, you pull out the instruction manual. So if you want to know how to have a great life, pull out the instruction manual—the Bible!

God made the world and everything in it so he knows how it works best. God gives us guidelines and principles to follow, and rules that tell us how to act and live for the best possible results.

For example, the Bible tells us not to lie because lying leads to trouble. When we lie, people eventually find out and stop trusting us. That wrecks our relationship with them. Lying spoils friendships and opportunities. To have a happy life, with good, trusting relationships and great opportunities, people need to trust us. We need to follow the rule not to lie. It's for our own good. The Bible also tells us how to handle our money, honor and be close to God, treat others, have good friendships, and much more.

Want a good life? Pull out the Instruction Manual. Follow it and you will have a good life. Guaranteed!

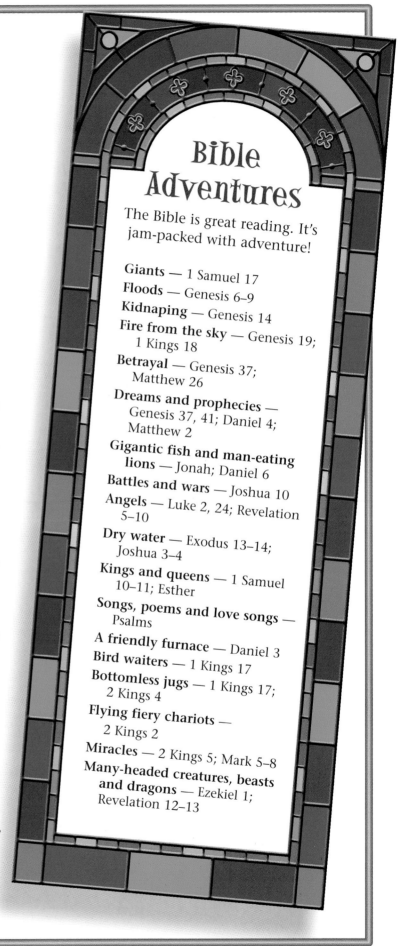

Bible Adventures

The Bible is great reading. It's jam-packed with adventure!

Giants — 1 Samuel 17

Floods — Genesis 6–9

Kidnaping — Genesis 14

Fire from the sky — Genesis 19; 1 Kings 18

Betrayal — Genesis 37; Matthew 26

Dreams and prophecies — Genesis 37, 41; Daniel 4; Matthew 2

Gigantic fish and man-eating lions — Jonah; Daniel 6

Battles and wars — Joshua 10

Angels — Luke 2, 24; Revelation 5–10

Dry water — Exodus 13–14; Joshua 3–4

Kings and queens — 1 Samuel 10–11; Esther

Songs, poems and love songs — Psalms

A friendly furnace — Daniel 3

Bird waiters — 1 Kings 17

Bottomless jugs — 1 Kings 17; 2 Kings 4

Flying fiery chariots — 2 Kings 2

Miracles — 2 Kings 5; Mark 5–8

Many-headed creatures, beasts and dragons — Ezekiel 1; Revelation 12–13

It's a Publishing Miracle!

Moses: *Prince, shepherd, leader—recognized as the writer of most of the Pentateuch, the first five books of the Bible.*

David: *Shepherd, musician, king—wrote many of the Psalms.*

Paul: *Religious leader—wrote about thirteen of the letters in the New Testament.*

Luke: *Medical doctor—wrote the books of Luke and Acts.*

John: *Fisherman—wrote the four books called John and Revelation.*

God is the Bible's author, but if you're picturing him typing away at a galaxy-sized computer, stop! That's not how he did it! He *inspired* the Bible. That means he worked with and through people, by his Holy Spirit, so that they wrote what he wanted. No other book has ever been written like this!

God chose people. Using their own personalities, ways of speaking, cultures and experiences, he got them to write down what he wanted to tell us. Every word they wrote is from God. "God has breathed life into all of Scripture" (2 Timothy 3:16). "No prophecy in Scripture ever came from a prophet's own understanding. It never came simply because a prophet wanted it to. Instead, the Holy Spirit guided the prophets as they spoke" (2 Peter 1:20-21).

God chose more than forty people to write the 66 books in the Bible. Some were rich; some were poor. There were kings, poets, prophets, prisoners, musicians, philosophers, generals, farmers, teachers, priests, politicians, shepherds, a tax collector, a doctor, and a couple of fishermen. The writers also spoke different languages (Hebrew, Aramaic, and Greek) and lived in different continents (Africa, Asia, and Europe) and at different times. It took over 1500 years to write the whole Bible!

Imagine getting forty people from different cultures, backgrounds, jobs, and times in history to agree on something as complicated as life, religion, and what's right and wrong! Yet the Bible's writers agree on all the main issues and more! In fact, what they wrote all fits together perfectly into the one big story of God's plan for us. Only God could have done that!

Copy Right!

The Bible was written long before paper was invented. The earliest "paper" was clay tablets. Later, dried animal skins called *parchment,* or sheets of *papyrus* made from grass-like papyrus plants were glued then rolled up into scrolls. Even later, parchment or papyrus pieces were sewn together like pages in a book.

The last book of the Bible was written 1350 years before the printing press was invented.

The Bible was copied by hand.

For all that time, books were copied by hand! This took such a long time that often a church or *synagogue* (a Jewish church) had only one copy of the Bible (or parts of it) to share.

The Jews knew the Bible was God's words and instructions. They treated the Old Testament with great respect. To keep the words correct they copied it *very* carefully. The *scribes* or copiers had rules about the kind of parchment and ink to use, how to space things, and how to ensure accuracy. They'd count the letters and words in their copies and compare them to what the rules said they should have. A copy with even one mistake was destroyed!

The New Testament copiers were non-Jews who didn't have as many rules to guide them. For hundreds of years, the job was done by monks in monasteries hunched over high desks in small, dimly lit rooms, called *scriptoriums.*

We can compare copies from different times and places and they're all the same!

בְּרֵאשִׁית בָּרָא אֱלֹהִים
אֵת הַשָּׁמַיִם וְאֵת הָאָרֶץ

The Old Testament was written right to left in Hebrew, with a few sections in Aramaic.

Οὕτως γὰρ ἠγάπησεν ὁ
θεὸς τὸν κόσμον, ὥστε

The New Testament was written in Greek like this, with a sprinkling of Aramaic words.

91

The Bible Is Amazing!

The Bible is one-of-a-kind! It was written in a way no ordinary book could possibly be written and still make sense. Here's why it's amazing:

It's Number One

The Bible has been read by more people, in more languages, than any other book. It was the first book to be printed on a printing press and one of the first to be translated into another language. Millions of Bibles are sold or given out every year around the world in 2000 languages and dialects.

It's the Best Kept

We have over 5000 old hand-written copies or parts of copies of the New Testament. We also have tens of thousands of pieces of copies of the Old Testament!

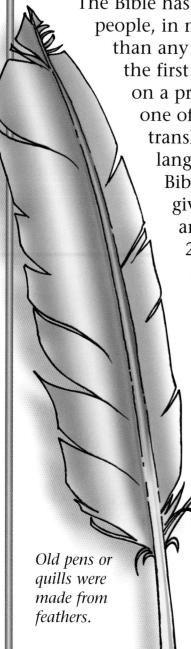

Old pens or quills were made from feathers.

They show that the Bible we have today is the same as when it was written!

It Tells It Like It Was

Many people have said the Bible couldn't be God's words because it's full of people and places they thought were made up. But, as archaeologists examine more old places, what the Bible says is shown to be completely right!

The Bible Is Accurate

How do we know that the copies of the Bible are accurate? We compare.

1. The older the *manuscript* is, the more accurate it is—it's been copied fewer times so there are fewer chances of mistakes.

2. When copies from many different places and times say the same things, it shows they're accurate.

Until 1947, our oldest piece of the Old Testament was from 800 years after Jesus. Then a shepherd boy in Israel found clay jars hidden in a cave. They contained what we call the *Dead Sea Scrolls*. Among them was a scroll of Isaiah from 200 years before Jesus! People compared this manuscript with what we already had—it's almost exactly the same!

We have over 5000 ancient copies or pieces of copies of the New Testament. We also have a whole New Testament from only 300 years after the last book was written!

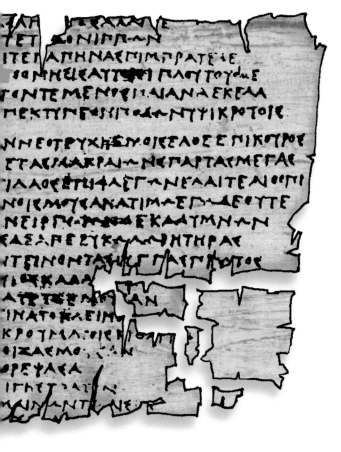

Ancient copies of the New Testament were words on papyrus like this.

It Tells It Like It Will Be

The Bible has a lot of prophecy in it. Prophecy is God telling us what's going to happen. Many prophecies in the Bible came true over a thousand years later! Only God knows the future.

The Bible is so completely one of a kind that no other book is even in the contest!

Monks copied the Scriptures by hand for hundreds of years.

From "ΑΓΑΠΗ" to "LOVE"

"Ουτωζ γαρ ηγαπησεν ο Θεος τον κοσμον." Or "Houtos (who-toes) gar agapasen (ay-gap-ay-sen) ho theos (thay-oss) ton (tone) kosmon (kosmoan)." **Say what?** Those are Jesus' words. You didn't recognize them? Well, they're in Greek. The story of how they got from that to "For God so loved the world" is fascinating!

The Old Testament was translated from Hebrew into Greek 200 years before Jesus by 70 scholars. It's called the *Septuagint* (meaning "seventy") or LXX (the Roman numeral for seventy). Since the New Testament was written in Greek too, most people could understand the whole Bible. But over the next several hundred years, Latin became the common language, and people couldn't read it as easily. So a man named Jerome made a translation into Latin. His translation, the *Vulgate,* was finished in A.D. 405.

Meanwhile, others were translating the Bible into their own languages such as Coptic, Syriac, Ethiopic, Gothic, and Armenian. Some languages had never been written before so translators even had to make up alphabets. In the late 1100s the Bible started to be translated into European languages, like Spanish and French.

For hundreds of years the authorities only allowed the clergy—priests and pastors—to have Bibles. In 1374 John Wycliffe said everyone should be able to read the Bible for themselves. His followers made the first English translation, the *Wycliffe Bible,* around 1395. The authorities were upset and made it illegal to own an English Bible without permission! But that didn't stop people—even though the translators were often jailed or killed.

Around 1456 the Bible was the first book printed on a printing press. Copies became cheaper to own, and Bibles were quickly printed in many different languages. Translations took off! In 1611 King James the First had the best Bible scholars put together the most famous English Bible, the *King James Version*.

There are several major English translations today: New International Version, New King James Version, New Revised Standard Version, and the New Living Translation.

By the end of 1995, at least part of the Bible had been translated into more than 2100 languages, the whole Bible had been translated into 276 languages, and more translations are still being made. The Bible is a worldwide book!

The first printed Bible was made on a printing press similar to this one.

The First Book Printed

A very famous man was born around A.D. 1400 (actually he wasn't famous yet) in Mainz, Germany. Johann Gutenberg was trained as a goldsmith, but he was tired of goldsmithing and was experimenting with printing. Printing at that time was done by cutting words and pictures into large wood blocks. The blocks were inked, and parchment, or the newly discovered paper, was pressed onto the ink.

Gutenberg had a better idea. He thought, "What if I cut each letter onto a separate piece of wood or metal? I could use the same pieces, or type, over and over. I could rearrange them into new words, sentences and pages. *Moveable type* would let me print better and cheaper books!" It was a revolutionary idea!

By 1456 he had printed the first ever books—around 180 *Gutenberg Bibles* in Latin—using moveable type.

His Bible was a great success and soon everyone was printing this same way!

What's in It?

The Gospels according to Matthew, Mark, Thomas . . . Hold it! There's no Gospel of Thomas, is there? Actually there is, but it's not in the Bible. It's not part of the *canon*—the books that are accepted as Scripture.

The Bible is made up of sixty-six books. Why only these? Well, God helped people recognize the books that were his.

The Old Testament

No one is sure how the canon of the Old Testament was decided. The *Pentateuch* or *The Law*—the first five books of the Bible—was recognized as belonging in the Bible more than 500 years before Jesus. *The Prophets* and *Psalms* were seen as canonical 100 to 200 years

before Jesus. Jesus talked about "the Law, the Prophets, and Psalms" as inspired by God and part of the Bible. Ninety years after Jesus' birth, a Jewish council declared the Old Testament canon to be what we have today.

Some copies of Bibles have other books in them called *The Apocrypha*. These books have good things in them, but they're not recognized as inspired by God or part of the canon.

The New Testament

After the Apostles died, all kinds of new writings claimed to be true. But some taught false things. The people needed to know what to believe, so the church

Can you find the books of the Bible in this library?

leaders had to discover which books and letters were from God. One of the keys in deciding was whether the book was known to have been written by an apostle or someone who worked closely with them, like Luke. As early as A.D. 170 the four Gospels (Matthew, Mark, Luke, and John) were recognized as canonical. Next were Paul's letters, then Revelation, Acts, and the letters of other apostles. In A.D. 367 an important pastor, Athanasius, wrote a letter listing the canon of the New Testament.

Just over 300 years after Jesus' death and resurrection, all the books of the Bible were the same as we have today. The canon was set and closed!

The Bible Library

Now what order should the books be in? Alphabetical? Longest to shortest or vice versa? Nope. How about topical? Sure! They did it like two libraries: Old Testament and New Testament. They put history first, then the other types of writing, then prophecy.

Here's the Old Testament Library—all the books of the law from Genesis to Deuteronomy. Then the history books, Joshua to Esther. After that, the poetic books, Job to the Song of Songs. Next come the major prophets with lots to say—Isaiah to Daniel—then the minor prophets with less to say—Hosea to Malachi. And that's how Christians organize the Old Testament.

The New Testament Library is similar. First come the history books, the Gospels and Acts. Then come the letters that were written during or after Acts. Paul's letters are first, then come Hebrews and the other letters. Finally, there's prophecy, the book of Revelation.

Old Testament Books

Law
Genesis
Exodus
Leviticus
Numbers
Deuteronomy

Historical
Joshua
Judges
Ruth
1&2 Samuel
1&2 Kings
1&2 Chronicles
Ezra
Nehemiah
Esther

Poetic
Job
Psalms
Proverbs
Ecclesiastes
Song of Songs

Major Prophets
Isaiah
Jeremiah
Lamentations
Ezekiel
Daniel

Minor Prophets
Hosea
Joel
Amos
Obadiah
Jonah
Micah
Nahum
Habakkuk
Zephaniah
Haggai
Zechariah
Malachi

New Testament Books

Historical
Matthew
Mark
Luke
John
Acts

Paul's Letters
Romans
1&2 Corinthians
Galatians
Ephesians
Philippians
Colossians
1&2 Thessalonians
1&2 Timothy
Titus
Philemon

Other Letters
Hebrews
James
1&2 Peter
1,2&3 John
Jude

Prophecy
Revelation

The Greatest Story

The Bible tells one big story about God creating everything so he could have a wonderful Father/child relationship with us. But everything was wrecked, so God put his plan into action to make it all better. Here's the story in a nutshell.

It began when only God existed—God the Father, Son, and Holy Spirit. God made everything! He made people, Adam and Eve, to be like his children. He wanted to be our Father and have a fantastic relationship with us. He gave Adam and Eve a beautiful Garden to live in with all good things, and one rule: Don't eat fruit from this one tree! But Satan, an important angel who became God's enemy, disguised himself and lied to them. They ate the fruit! That was sin, so God sent them out of the Garden. Sin separates us from God. As a result, everyone born since then has been born sinful and separated from God too. Satan and sin spoiled God's plan to be a father to us. But don't worry. The story is just beginning!

Adam and Eve had children who had children. . . . Soon the world was full of sinful people. God was very sad. He said, "I'll destroy everyone." But God found one man who loved him, Noah. God told Noah to build a huge boat or *ark*. He sent two of every animal into the ark with Noah's family. It began to rain. We're talking **RAIN**! Forty days and nights later, only those in the ark were alive.

Noah's children had children who. . . . God chose Noah's descendant Abraham with his wife Sarah. He told them he'd be their God and sent them to a land he promised to give their children forever. Off they went to Canaan. But Abraham and Sarah couldn't have children. Then God gave them a son, Isaac, and promised that one of his descendants (the *Messiah*) would bless the whole world!

Isaac's son Jacob, or *Israel*, had twelve sons and one daughter. Jacob gave his favorite son Joseph a special coat. Joseph's brothers were jealous. They sold him as a slave into Egypt.

Adam and Eve sin

God gives Abraham and Sarah a son

Joseph's family come to Egypt

Joseph kept loving and obeying God. Years later God helped him explain a dream to the *Pharaoh* or king of Egypt—a huge famine was coming! Pharaoh told Joseph to get Egypt ready. When Joseph's family came for food, Joseph invited them to live in Egypt.

The *Israelites*, all Israel's descendants, came and had children who had children who. . . . They increased until the new Pharaoh got worried. He made them slaves and ordered their baby boys killed. That's when Pharaoh's daughter rescued an Israelite baby, Moses. Moses grew up in the palace, then he ran away to the desert. Years later he saw a bush burning without burning up. God spoke to him from it, "Go to Egypt. Tell Pharaoh to let my people go!" God sent ten plagues to show he was stronger than Egypt's false gods. In the last plague the eldest child in every family was to die. But the Israelites killed lambs and put the blood on their doorways so God would pass over their houses. The lambs died instead of the eldest children. This was called the *Passover*. That night Pharaoh let God's people go!

The Israelites left in a huge *Exodus*. God led them into the desert and gave Moses the *Ten Commandments* and the Law telling them how to please God and have a good life. Then God led them to the land he'd promised Abraham long ago. Under the leader Joshua, the Israelites defeated the wicked people living there and settled in. When the Israelites followed God's Law, things went well. When they didn't, their enemies conquered them. They'd cry to God for help, and God would send a judge or leader to defeat their enemies. One judge, Deborah, told Barak to gather an army to fight Commander Sisera. The army defeated the enemy! Another judge was Samson. God gave him amazing strength. Alone, he killed 1000 men who came to capture him!

Years later the Israelites asked God for a king. Their first king, Saul, fought their enemies, the Philistines. A giant Philistine, Goliath, mocked God. Young David fought him with a sling and stones. He won! He loved God with all his heart. His son Solomon was wise, but later

The Israelites leave Egypt

The Israelites conquer Canaan

David fights Goliath

God saves Daniel from the lions

Jesus is born in a stable

Jesus heals the sick

kings didn't love God like David did. God sent *prophets* to remind his people to follow his Law. They didn't listen. So God let enemies take them prisoner far away to Babylon.

Daniel was an Israelite or *Jew* who loved God and became a leader in Babylon. He prayed to God even when it was against Babylon's law. So he was thrown into a lions' den. But God kept Daniel safe! Later, the ruler let some Jews return to their land. Now God's people decided to obey God's Law. Everything was ready for the key part of God's plan!

God sent an angel to Mary and her fiancé, Joseph, saying Mary would have God's baby. Mary had a little boy, *Jesus*, just as God had said. Jesus was God, but he became a person like us because he loved us. He was part of God's plan—the promised Messiah. God told simple Jewish shepherds and non-Jewish wise men about his Son's birth, showing he'd come for *everyone*.

Jesus grew up in Nazareth. When he was about thirty, he began the job God had given him. At the Jordan River he was baptized. Then God led him into the desert. Satan tempted Jesus to do things his way instead of God's, just like he had done to Adam and Eve. But Jesus quoted from the Bible and refused.

Jesus taught about God and his kingdom. He showed that God loved people by healing the sick and feeding the hungry. He taught how to have a good relationship with God. Jesus chose twelve

A horrible death

Saul meets Jesus

Jesus is coming back

men to be his special followers or *disciples*. The religious leaders were afraid the crowds would follow Jesus instead of them because he taught new ideas like,"God loved the world so much that he gave his one and only Son. Anyone who believes in him will not die but will have eternal life" (John 3:16). The leaders thought the key was to obey the Law, not believe in Jesus. They decided to get rid of Jesus but were afraid of a riot.

Judas, one of Jesus' disciples, offered to help the leaders arrest Jesus. Around the time of the Passover celebration (remember the Passover?) Judas led guards to arrest Jesus. Jesus was tried for saying he was God's Son. The punishment was death. Jesus was beaten and led out to be crucified, a horrible death. Jesus asked his Father to forgive the people because they didn't know what they were doing. Then he said, "It's finished." He'd done everything God sent him to do!

After he died, friends put his body in a tomb. The Romans guarded the tomb so no one could steal Jesus' body and say he'd risen from the dead. But on the third day the tomb was empty! Jesus appeared to many people, proving he was alive again.

God had accepted his death (instead of ours) as payment for our sins! That meant the separation begun by Adam and Eve was ended. All people could be God's children!

Jesus sent the Holy Spirit to help his followers tell the world about him. The Jewish leaders tried to stop them, but nothing worked. One leader, Saul, searched out Jesus' followers to have them killed. One day Jesus appeared to Saul and asked why he was persecuting God's people. From that day Saul changed his name to Paul. Paul traveled around the world telling people about Jesus. He started churches and wrote letters to help new believers live as God wanted. He also explained the teachings of the Bible and Jesus.

John, another disciple, was sent to an island prison for following Jesus. Jesus gave him a message for the Church. It's in *Revelation* in our Bible. Jesus promised to come back and take us to be with him in a new heaven and earth. There'll be love and happiness there. No more sadness or pain! We'll be with God as his children just as he planned before the world began. What a party that will be!

The Bible tells the best story ever written. And every part is true!

Archaeology Digs It

Imagine this: 300 years from now no one believes there is a place called California and no one has heard of Walt Disney! Let's say just one book talks about California. Because there's so little evidence people don't believe the writer. Then someone starts digging and finds Magic Mountain! They find other books about California and pictures of Walt Disney. Now they believe the writer and they take her seriously.

That's what happened with the Bible. For a long time, it was the only book that talked about certain places and people, so scholars didn't believe that those people or places ever existed. Then along came *archaeologists* who study anything old to learn about the past. In the last eighty years, they have found other writings mentioning the same things as the Bible. They have also dug up ancient ruins that confirm what the Bible says.

Wherever people live they leave things behind—clay pots, weapons, writing, and buildings. Some of these things are kept safe in the ground for *thousands* of years. By studying these ancient things, archaeologists learn about their owners.

They might study a hill. Long before it was a hill, people built a town there. Over time, dirt, garbage, and new building projects added layers. Maybe the town was destroyed by enemies. Another town was built on the ruins. Archaeologists dig down through the hill's layers, often finding several towns built on top of each other. Archaeologists compare what they find with things from other places. They discover when the things were made, who lived there and for how long, who they did business with, and so on.

Thousands of sites have been excavated all over Bible lands. And guess what! **Nothing** has been found to prove the Bible wrong! Nada! Zilch! Zero!

Archeologists use tools like these to uncover ancient towns.

Digs like this teach us about the past.

Digging Up the Truth

Check out what people used to think and what archaeologists have found!

☞ **Thought:** Moses couldn't have written the first Bible books (Deuteronomy 31:24) because in his time, no one knew how to write yet.

Found: A "Black Stele" (a carved black rock) three hundred years older than Moses' time with laws written on it. Also, tablets from the excavated city of Ebla written a thousand years before Moses.

☞ **Thought:** There was no Sodom, Gomorrah, and other cities Genesis says were in the Jordan valley. No one lived there in Abraham's time.

Found: The Ebla tablets mention the same cities in the same order as Genesis 14. And ruins of more than seventy towns and cities from Abraham's time and older have been found there.

Scholars translate ancient writing on clay tablets like this.

☞ **Thought:** The Hittites (Genesis 23:10; Joshua 11:1–9) didn't exist.

Found: A Hittite city and tablets from Egypt that mention the Hittites.

☞ **Thought:** Joshua didn't really conquer Canaan (Joshua 10–11). He and the Israelites moved in peacefully.

Found: Tablets from Canaan kings asking Egypt for help against Habiru (Hebrew) invaders.

☞ **Thought:** Pontius Pilate wasn't a real person. If he was, he shouldn't have been called "Prefect."

Found: A large stone saying, "Pontius Pilate, Prefect of Judea."

☞ **Thought:** King David was a legend. He didn't really exist.

Found: An inscription from David's time that refers to the "House of David" and the "King of Israel."

There are many other examples of things being found that agree with what the Bible says.

Parts adapted with permission from Josh McDowell's books A Ready Defense *and* More Evidence That Demands a Verdict.

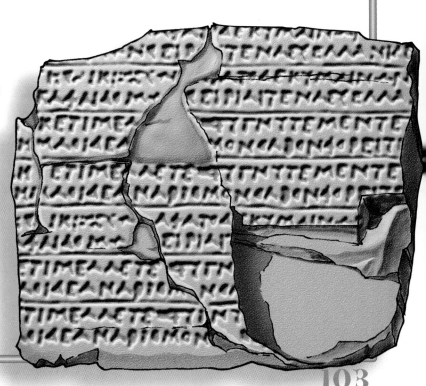

God's Treasure Map

A copper scroll was found with the *Dead Sea Scrolls*. It described *treasures* hidden around the countryside! The experts studied it to make sure it was for real and to figure out exactly where the treasures should be.

Landmarks have changed over the 2000 years since the scroll was written, so the experts also studied other scrolls and histories to help them compare how things *were* to how they *are* now. They probably copied and memorized the scroll's clues and directions so they'd have the information even when they were away from the scroll.

The Bible is just like the copper treasure scroll. It was written by someone who knows what he's talking about—God! He made life and knows how it works. He knows how to help us find the life-treasures he's prepared for us—things like good families, friendships, happiness, freedom, safety, success, and comfort. He gave us a "scroll" with everything we need to find his treasures for a great life. Just as we'd study an ancient scroll or map, we can study God's map.

"God has breathed life into all of Scripture. It is useful for teaching us what is true . . . for correcting our mistakes . . . making our lives whole again . . . training us to do what is right. By using Scripture, [God's people] can be completely prepared to do every good thing" (2 Timothy 3:16–17). Here's how to learn from God's "treasure map."

Read

The experts had to read the scroll to understand what it was about. Reading the whole Bible helps us understand what God and his book are all about. It gives us the overall story of God's plan and why Jesus came. It also shows us who God is and what he's like.

Study

The experts' second step was to study the scroll. They spent time with it, looked at it in sections, and did whatever else would help them understand it. They'd study one particular treasure, find out all about it, and make sure they understood the instructions.

We can use the Bible the same way. We can pick a topic we need to know more about. We can study that topic by looking up the places in the Bible that talk about it. By studying the Bible we can understand *why* God says things like, "Be honest. Use words to encourage, not destroy." We'll discover all kinds of things!

Memorize

The experts probably memorized key parts of the scroll. That way they could refer to them when they were out hunting for the treasure. We memorize Bible verses for the same reason. We need to know how to find the treasure in any situation and do the right thing. For example, say you get upset and say unkind things. That's definitely not a treasure! Want the treasure of a great friendship? Memorize Ephesians 4:29: "Say only what will help to build others up and meet their needs. Then what you say will help those who listen." Now the

next time you're tempted to be unkind with your words you'll know what to do. And hey! Your friendship becomes even better—a treasure!

You see, the Bible is not a book just for knowledge. No way! It's a book for living. It's real. God's treasure map is there for us to use and learn from. So read, study, memorize—and keep digging up treasures!

No matter what your age or your style, there's a Bible out there to make you smile.

Read the Treasure Map

When you learn to sing you begin with "do, re, mi." What about when you start reading the Bible? Well, starting at the beginning is a very good place to start! But remember, the Bible is like a library. Don't try to take on the whole library in one go! Tackle one book at a time.

There are lots of ways to read the Bible.

You might start by reading the Old Testament history books Genesis and Exodus. Then read the New Testament history books Luke and Acts. Then go to one of the letters. A good one is James. These books will give you an overview of God's plan.

First Find Plan

Introduction to the Bible

This plan is your first look at the Bible's treasures. It's good for those who haven't really read the Bible before.

Beginnings
Genesis

Forming a Nation
Exodus

Jesus' Story
Luke

The Church Begins
Acts

Practical Living
James

Treasure Trove

Digging Deeper

For serious treasure hunters. This plan hits the treasure payload and is a good expansion of the First Find Plan.

Numbers 8–27
Deuteronomy 6, 7, 34
Joshua 1–10, 24
Judges 1–7, 13–16
Ruth
1 Samuel 1–21, 23–31
2 Samuel 5–7
Psalms 23, 32, 100, 103, 130, 139
1 Kings 3–5, 8–12
Proverbs 1–3, 10, 15
1 Kings 16–18
2 Kings 2–5, 7, 12, 18–20, 22–24
Isaiah 53 (It's about Jesus' job)
Jeremiah 52:1–16
Daniel 1–6
2 Chronicles 36:22–23
Ezra 1, 3, 6
Nehemiah 1–8
Esther

John
Acts (If it's been a while, you might want to read Acts again.)
Romans 1–8, 12–14
1 Corinthians 12–15
2 Corinthians 4–5, 9
Galatians 5–6
Ephesians 4–6
Philippians 2–4
1 Thessalonians 4–5
1 Timothy 6
2 Timothy 2, 4
Titus 3
Hebrews 11
1 Peter 1–3
2 Peter 3
1 John
Revelation 1–3, 20–22

We read the Bible to help us grow in a relationship with God. Since the Bible is God's book, spending time reading the Bible is spending time with God. By reading it daily, we're getting in touch with him and getting to know him.

You see, the Bible is no ordinary book! Oh no! The Holy Spirit, who helped God's chosen writers say what God wanted, is still working through the Bible. He can make it come alive to us. No, it won't get up and walk around or do flips. But it just might "talk." The Holy Spirit helps us understand what the words and stories mean. The Bible "comes alive" because the Holy Spirit uses it to say something we need to hear, answer a question we have, or help us understand just what we're going through. God "breathes" into our lives through his words in the Bible. This makes the Bible totally unique: God uses the words written thousands of years ago to help us in our lives *today*. That's one of the Holy Spirit's jobs! (Remember 2 Timothy 3:16–17?)

We've given you some Bible reading plans. Also, if you want to jump around in the Bible a bit and read some favorite parts, check out pages 108–109. They tell you where to find the famous stuff in the Bible. Choose your plan, and happy treasure hunting!

Treasure Teasers

Bible hot spots.

Sssmoking!
Jeremiah 36

The Sword
Ephesians 6:10-18

Kings Please Leaf
Judges 9:1-15

Clouds in Church
Exodus 40:1-2, 17-38

No Sleeping in Church
Acts 20:7-12

House Cleaning
Mark 11:15-19

Longest, Loudest Church
Revelation 4-5

Plagues
Exodus 7:8-12:30

Spies
Numbers 13

Noses and Toeses
1 Corinthians 12

The Best of the Bible

Think of your favorite book or story. You probably know it pretty well. And you probably have favorite parts too, parts you love hearing over and over and over again. Well, the Bible's been around a l-o-o-o-n-g time! In that time people have had many favorite parts. Some of them become favorites for just about everyone. Here are some of the all-time favorites!

Famous Old Testament Verses

The Shepherd's Psalm
Psalm 23
Thanks Psalm
Psalm 100
God Knows You
Psalm 139
Seek Wisdom
Proverbs 2:3–4
Trust God
Proverbs 3:5–6
Wise Request
1 Kings 3:1–15
Time for Everything
Ecclesiastes 3:1–8
Jesus Will Suffer
Isaiah 52:13–53:12
Let's Talk
Isaiah 1:18
The Christmas Verse
Isaiah 9:6
Good Plans for You
Jeremiah 29:11–14

Famous New Testament Verses

The Blesseds
Matthew 5:1–12
Don't Worry
Matthew 6:25–34
Great Commands
Mark 12:28–34
Nicodemus's Lesson
John 3:16
Rest for the Weary
Matthew 11:28–30
Spirit Fruit
Galatians 5:22–26
Love's the Thing
1 Corinthians 13
Body Parts
1 Corinthians 12:12–31
Spiritual Armor
Ephesians 6:10–18
God Dries Tears
Revelation 21:1–5

The Lord's Prayer

Our Father in heaven, may your name be honored.
May your kingdom come.
May what you want to happen be done on earth as it is done in heaven.
Give us today our daily bread.
Forgive us our sins, just as we also have forgiven those who sin against us.
Keep us from falling into sin when we are tempted.
Save us from the evil one.

(Matthew 6:9–13)

The Ten C

1. Don't put any other gods in place of me.

2. Don't make any statues of gods. . . . Don't bow down and worship them.

3. Don't misuse the name of the Lord your God.

4. Remember to keep the Sabbath day holy.

5. Honor your father and mother.

Famous Bible Stories

Remember what we said about God's reasons for giving us the Bible? The Bible is full of exciting, fascinating stories to read and enjoy. But they're there for another reason, too. They teach us how life works, what happens when we obey God or when we don't, the power of prayer, how God cares for us . . . and on and on it goes! So here are some great stories. Enjoy them and find the treasure in them that God has for you.

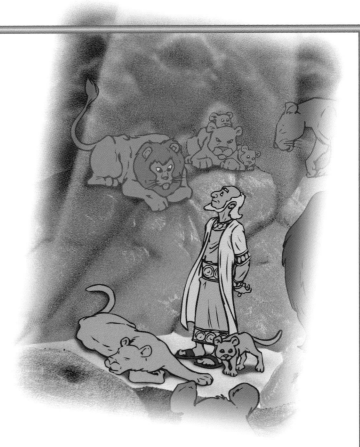

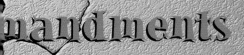

mandments

6. **Don't commit murder.**

7. **Don't commit adultery.**

8. **Don't steal.**

9. **Don't give false witness against your neighbor.**

10. **Don't long for or envy anything that belongs to your neighbor.**

Study the Treasure Map

Okay! You're reading the Bible and discovering what this "treasure scroll" is all about. Ready for serious digging? Want to discover specific treasures, like how to pray? or have great friendships?

Think of our copper roll expert. He or she studies, cross-checks, then acts: off for the treasure! Ready to try it? Let's do a *topical study*.

1 Get a notebook and call it your *Treasure Chest*. You'll fill it with the gold and jewels you find in the Bible!

2 Choose a "treasure" to study, say *love*.

3 Pray. God understands his book better than anyone. So it's important to ask for his help.

4 Find a part of the Bible that teaches about your topic. A great section on love is 1 Corinthians 13. Read it. Think about it. Ask questions. For example, what does "is not self-seeking" mean? Write down your thoughts.

Everything in the Bible fits together, and the Bible has oodles to say about love. Let's check it out by using some *tools of the trade*.

5 Many Bibles have *cross-references*, little notes beside verses that point to other verses on the same topic. In our picture, look up the cross-references for 1 Corinthians 13:5. You can follow the topic's trail from verse to verse like following a trail in the woods. Try 1 Corinthians 10:24 too. What does "is not self-seeking" mean?

Cross Reference

1 CORINTHIANS 13:1

Love

And now I will show you the most excellent way.

13 If I speak in the tongues of men and of angels, but have not love, I am only a resounding gong or a clanging symbol. ²If I have the gift of prophecy and can fathom all mysteries and all knowledge, and if I have faith that can move mountains, but have not love, I am nothing. ³If I give all I possess to the poor and surrender my body to the flames, but not have love, I gain nothing.

13:1	ver 8; S Mk 16:17
13:2	ver 8; S Eph 4:11; S Ac 11:27
	1Co 14:2
	S 2Co 8:7
	1Co 12:9
	Mt 17:20; 21:21
13:3	Lk 19:8; S Ac 2:45
	Da 3:28
13:4	1Th 5:14
	1Co 5:2
13:5	
	S 1Co 10:24
	S Mt 5:22; Job 14:16,17; Pr 10:12;17:9; 1Pe 4:8
13:6	2Th 2:12
	2Jn 4; 3Jn 3,4
13:7	ver 8, 13

⁴Love is patient, love is kind. It does not envy, it does not boast, it is not proud. ⁵It is not rude, it is not self-seeking, it is not easily angered, it keeps no record of wrongs. ⁶Love does not delight in evil but rejoices with the truth. ⁷It always protects, always trusts, always hopes, always perseveres.

⁸Love never fails. But where there are prophecies, they will cease; where there are tongues, they will be stilled; where there is knowledge, it will pass away. ⁹For we know in part and we prophesy in part, ¹⁰but when

6 A *concordance*. Most Bibles have a small one in the back. Concordances list Bible words, and verses that use them. From our pic-

Concordance

LOVE (BELOVED LOVED LOVELY LOVER LOVER'S LOVERS LOVES LOVING LOVING-KINDNESS)

Ge	20: 13	'This is how you can show your *l*
	22: 2	your only son, Isaac, whom you *l,*
	29:18	Jacob was in *l* with Rachel and said
	29:20	days to him because of his *l* for her
	29:32	Surely my husband will *l* me now."
Ex	15:13	"In your unfailing *l* you will lead
	20: 6	showing *l* to a thousand generations
	20: 6	of those who *l* me
	21: 5	'I *l* my master and my wife
	34: 6	abounding in *l* and faithfulness.
	34: 7	maintaining *l* to thousands.
Lev	19:18	but *l* your neighbor as yourself.
	19:34	*L* him as yourself,
Nu	14:18	abounding in *l* and forgiving sin
	14:19	In accordance with your great *l,*
Dt.	5:10	showing *l* to a thousand generations
	5:10	to those that *l* me
	6: 5	*L* the LORD your God
	7: 9	generations of those who *l* him
	7: 9	keeping his covenant of *l*

Mt	3:17	"This is my Son, whom I *l;*
	5:43	'*L* your neighbor and hate your
	5:44	*L* your enemies and pray
	5:46	you *l* those who *l* you, what reward
	6: 5	for they *l* to pray standing
	6:24	he will hate the one and *l* the other
	12:18	the one I *l,* in whom I delight;
	17: 5	"This is my Son, whom I *l;*
	19:19	and '*l* your neighbor as yourself.'
	22:37	'*L* the Lord your God
Ro	5: 5	because God has poured out his *l*
	5: 8	God demonstrates his own *l* for us
	8:28	for the good of those who *l* him.
	8:35	us from the *l* of Christ?
	8:39	us from the *l* of God that is
	12: 9	*L* must be sincere.
	12:10	to one another in brotherly *l.*
	16: 8	Greet Ampiatus, whom I *l*
1 Co	2: 9	prepared for those who *l* him" –
	4:17	my son whom I *l,* who is faithful
	4:21	or in *l* and with a gentle spirit?
	8: 1	Knowledge puffs up, but *l* builds up
	13: 1	have not *l,* I am only a resounding
	13: 2	but have not *l,* I am nothing

ture, look up a couple of verses. Read the verses around them to see how they fit into what the writer is saying. Who is loving? How is love shown? Write your answers in your *Treasure Chest.*

7 *Bible dictionaries* are tools too. Like concordances, they're alphabetical and easy to use. Just look up "love" and there you are, love stuff. (Check out our picture.) If you're into computers you'll strike gold! Many study tools are on disc or CD ROM. Do a *search* or *find* on "love" and just see what the

computer kicks onto your screen!

Dig deep. Treasures are there for the taking!

8 *Act!* Now you get to live out what you've learned. God is ready to help.

Bible Dictionary

Love

LOVE

Love is the grandest theme of Scripture. It is a divine motivation. It moved God to reach out to the lost; and it enables the lost to look up in response, as well as to reach out to others. What the Bible says about love cannot help but enrich our lives.

OT   1. The Hebrew words
      2. God's love for man
      3. Man's love for God
NT   4. The Greek words
      5. God's love in Christ
      6. Man's love for God

8. Summary. God is portrayed in Scripture as the one who, moved by love, initiates a relationship with human beings. God's love prompts his free decision to reach out to sinful humanity.

In the OT, God's love is focused on the covenant people of Israel, and his love is demonstrated by his acts for them. In return, God's OT people are called to show their love for God by commitment to him alone and by obedience to his commands.

In the NT, the full scope and meaning of God's love is unveiled.

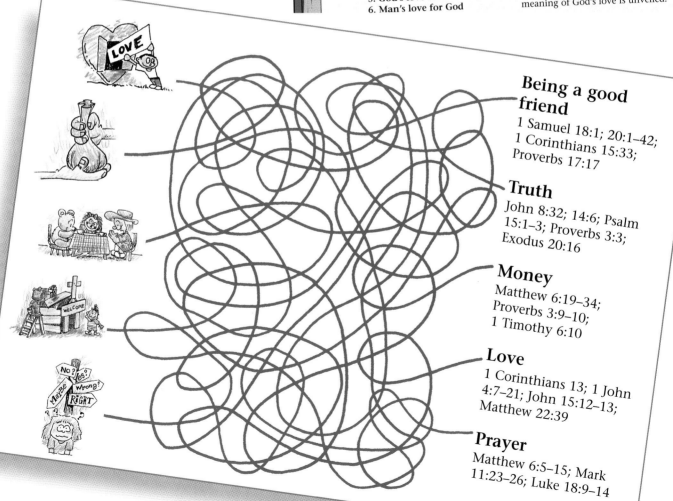

Being a good friend
1 Samuel 18:1; 20:1–42;
1 Corinthians 15:33;
Proverbs 17:17

Truth
John 8:32; 14:6; Psalm
15:1–3; Proverbs 3:3;
Exodus 20:16

Money
Matthew 6:19–34;
Proverbs 3:9–10;
1 Timothy 6:10

Love
1 Corinthians 13; 1 John
4:7–21; John 15:12–13;
Matthew 22:39

Prayer
Matthew 6:5–15; Mark
11:23–26; Luke 18:9–14

Learn It by Heart

Combination locks. Telephone numbers. Birth dates. What do these have in common? They're all things we memorize—with good reason. We do it so we can get into our lockers, call home and friends, and remember the special days of people we love.

The Bible is the same. We memorize parts of it for very good reasons. When we're out living, things come up that we need help with. We can't always get to life's instruction manual to look them up. But if we have verses in our heads and hearts we can find them quickly and *eureka!* We know what to do. We can apply the Bible's instructions right there and then.

Sunday schools often have contests and prizes for the most verses memorized. But don't forget the *reason* we memorize. It's not just to get points or win contests. Nope. It's much more important than that!

The world can be a dark place, with confusion, questions, sin, temptation, and disappointments. There are lots of choices to make, lots of paths to take. Which one is right? Which leads to God's treasure? If the paths are all dark it's hard to see which is safe or which has rocks and holes. Enter the Bible! God calls it a light. "Your word is like a lamp that shows me the way. It is like a light that guides me" (Psalm 119:105). The Bible can show us the right choice to make, the path that leads to a treasure. Memorizing key verses keeps that light right where we need it, in our hearts and heads. It helps us know the best way to live.

So let's memorize and light our lamp!

Memory Tips

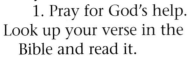

The key isn't just to memorize the words. It's the *meaning* you want. Here are some steps once you've chosen your verse:

1. Pray for God's help. Look up your verse in the Bible and read it.

2. Think about what the verse means.

3. Read it again. Think of where you could use it. At home? With friends? Doing schoolwork? On the playing field? With your piggy bank?

4. Read the verse again. You want to get the verse inside you, into your heart and your thinking. You want it to be part of you so that when a situation comes up you can pull it out of your brain's filing cabinet right away.

5. Read the verse a few more times out loud so you can hear it.

6. Close your Bible and say it out loud without looking.

7. Do this until you feel it's in your heart and you know where you can use it.

There you are! You have a jewel locked away in your mind/heart treasure chest. Now you simply review the verse every once in a while and ask God to remind you of it when you need it.

You're on the path to a treasure-filled life!

Memory Jewels

Friendship — Proverbs 17:17 "A friend loves at all times. He is there to help when trouble comes."

Temptation — 1 Corinthians 10:13 "You are tempted in the same way all other human beings are. God is faithful. He will not let you be tempted any more than you can take. But when you are tempted, God will give you a way out so that you can stand up under it."

Kids and Parents — Ephesians 6:1–3 "Children, obey your parents as believers in the Lord. Obey them because it's the right thing to do. Scripture says, 'Honor your father and mother.' That is the first commandment that has a promise. 'Then things will go well with you. You will live a long time on the earth.'"

How You Talk — Ephesians 4:29 "Don't let any evil talk come out of your mouths. Say only what will help to build others up and meet their needs. Then what you say will help those who listen."

When You Need Wisdom — James 1:5 "If any of you need wisdom, ask God for it. He will give it to you. God gives freely to everyone. He doesn't find fault."

When You Mess Up — 1 John 1:9 "But God is faithful and fair. If we admit that we have sinned, he will forgive us our sins. He will forgive every wrong thing we have done. He will make us pure."

The Life-Changing Book

The treasures we find in the Bible can change our lives. As we learn to live by its instructions, we become more like Jesus. And Jesus promised us a helper, the Holy Spirit, who would teach us about God and help us obey him.

Jesus died for our sins so that we could have God as our loving heavenly Father. When we pray and ask God to forgive us, he does. Then, with the help of the Holy Spirit and God's grace, we become more like he wants. That's what the Bible is all about.

Q Does the Bible tell us what God wants us to do?

A Yes. In the Bible, God's Word, God tells us what he wants us to do and how he wants us to live. Although there are a lot of stories and information in the Bible, God's four main instructions for our lives are: (1) believe in Jesus and trust him every day, (2) obey Jesus and do what he says, (3) love God and others, (4) be fair and honest and live for God without being proud about it.

Q Will people write about us in a special Bible, too?

A There is only one Bible (or "revelation from God"), and it has already been written. But remember, the Bible is far more than a collection of stories about people who lived a long time ago— it's God's message about Jesus; it tells how we should live today. The Bible also tells us about the future, not just the past. So in one sense, we are in the Bible. We are important in God's plan. Also, the Bible tells us that those who believe in Jesus have their names written in the "Lamb's Book of Life"— that's another book that God has. It tells who will live with God in heaven.

Q **Why do we study the Bible?**

A It's important to study the Bible because the Bible is God's message to us and studying it helps us understand it better. If you want to learn more about basketball, you study basketball. Studying the Bible helps us find out how to live and what God wants. When we only read the Bible (without studying it), we may not see the meaning right away. Studying helps us learn lessons for life. We learn God's will so we can obey him. Studying the Bible is like reading a story many, many times. Each time you see something different and learn more.

Q **What is the Bible's biggest story?**

A The biggest story is the story of Jesus. In fact, the whole Bible tells his story about God creating people and saving them from sin. Jesus came to the world to die in our place and pay the penalty for our sins. If we trust in Jesus as Savior, God gives us eternal life. The Old Testament Bible writers told us that Jesus would be born, live, die, and rise again. Even the sacrifices described in the book of Leviticus show us what the death of Christ would be, the perfect "Lamb of God who takes away the sin of the world." No matter where you look in the Bible, you can learn about Jesus. Have you put your faith in him?

Adapted from *101 Questions Children Ask About God*, Tyndale House Publishers, 1992 and *102 Questions Children Ask About the Bible*, Tyndale House Publishers, 1994. Used by permission.

The Best Way of All

God gave us the Bible so we could know him, learn his plan, and have great lives!

Remember, God is love. First Corinthians 13 (remember the study?) says that love is never selfish. So everything in God's book is for our good, not his. When God tells us to be honest (Proverbs 10:9), honesty makes our lives better. Loving God with all our hearts (Deuteronomy 6:5) makes us happier. Honoring our parents (Ephesians 6:1–3) means things will go well with us. The key to a happy life is obeying God. That doesn't mean we'll never be sad. But God will always be with us, helping us to learn and make it through.

Check out Psalm 119. It's all about the good things that come from loving and obeying God's Word. "Teach me to live as you command, because that makes me very happy" (Psalm 119:35). God doesn't tell us to study his book because there's a test. He tells us to do it because it has everything we need for fulfilled, happy, contented lives—in every part of our lives from home to school, sports to money, friends to feelings. What a great deal!

Questions and Activities

Pages 88-91

Learn It

1. What are four ways of describing the Bible?

   _____,

   _____,

   _____,

   _____.

2. How many people did it take to write the Bible?
   a. exactly 4
   b. more than 40
   c. only 1
   d. about 100

3. Choose the type of person below who *did not* help write the Bible:
   a. prisoner
   b. plumber
   c. farmer
   d. shepherd

4. How long did it take to write the Bible?
   a. less than 15 years
   b. just 150 years
   c. over 1,500 years
   d. exactly 15,000 years

5. What would the scribes do if they made a mistake while copying the Bible?
   a. burn their pens
   b. destroy the copy with the mistake on it
   c. run around the temple 10 times
   d. resign from their position

Think About It

1. Get out a fairly simple jigsaw puzzle, a small, unassembled Lego™ vehicle, or some other simple model. Dump the pieces on the table, then put away the box or the instructions so you can't see them. Now try and assemble the puzzle or model. Give yourself a time limit of five minutes.

   Afterward, answer the following questions:

   What was it like having to work without instructions?

   Would you rather work with the instructions or without them?

   What do you think our lives are like when we don't look at God's instructions in the Bible?

   How can God's instructions help you?

Play It

1. **Scribe for a Day**
   As you read in this book, the scribes who copied the Bible had to be very careful not to make any mistakes because they didn't want to distort the original words of the Bible. This may not sound too difficult, but it was not an easy task. Here's a fun activity that will show you how difficult it was.

   Take a fresh piece of paper and write a passage (about three or four verses) from the Bible at the top. Take the paper in turns to your siblings, parents, and friends and ask each one to carefully copy the proverb onto the paper. Only the first person copies your original.

Each person copies the one the person before them wrote. Ask them to try to match both the content and the style of your original writing.

When you have 10 or more copies, study the different versions carefully and see how closely they match the original. Can you spot any changes in the wording, spelling, or style of writing? How did the final message compare with the one that you started with? Why do you think it was different/the same? How is this exercise like the way the Scriptures were copied? How is it different?

Pages 92–95

Learn It

1. How many languages and dialects has the Bible been translated into?
   a. 100
   b. 6,000
   c. 10,000
   d. 2,000

2. How do prophecies show us that the Bible is true and is God's book?

   _____

   _____.

3. What are the Dead Sea Scrolls?
   a. a type of fish found only in the Dead Sea
   b. ancient copies of the Old Testament books found in caves near the Dead Sea
   c. an ancient traveler's guide to the Dead Sea area
   d. a history of the Dead Sea which explains why all the creatures in the Dead Sea died

4. Fill in the blanks with the following name from Bible copying and printing

history: *Vulgate, Wycliffe Bible, King James Bible, John Wycliffe, Gutenberg Bible, Septuagint, Johann Gutenberg, 70 scholars, Jerome.*

The _____ is a Greek translation of the Old Testament made by _____ 200 years before Jesus. The _____ is a Latin translation of the Bible made by _____ in 405 A.D. In 1395 _____'s followers made the first English translation of the Bible, called the _____.

The _____ is the most famous English translation of the Bible, published in 1611. In 1456 _____ printed the first book using moveable type. This book was called the _____.

Think About It

1. Why do you think only priests and pastors were allowed to read the Bible? How would you feel if you weren't allowed to read the Bible?

2. In this section you read that the first book Johann Gutenberg printed on his new printing press was the Bible. If the printing press was just invented this week, what do you think would be the first book printed? Do you think it would be the Bible? Why or why not?

3. How does learning about the extreme care people took to translate and copy the Bible properly affect the way you feel about it?

Do It

1. As you read in this book, the Bible was written by dozens of people from different countries and walks of life over hundreds of years, and yet every book of the Bible agrees with all of the rest. How was God able to get so many different people to agree on so many things? Just to get a feel for how difficult this was, conduct the following survey among your friends and family over the next week. Ask them the following questions and record their answers in a notebook.

   If there are aliens, what do you think they look like?

   What is the best dessert?

   What is the best show on television?

   Who is the best music group?

   What's the first thing you would buy if you won one million dollars?

   What are the two most important rules of life?

Once you've completed your survey, examine their answers. How are they the same? How are they different? Chances are, hardly anyone answered the questions the same way. If you think getting a few people from the same culture and time in history to share the same opinion on a few simple topics is difficult, try to imagine how God did it with the Bible, which deals with hundreds of important topics. You'll probably agree that it must have taken a miracle—and it did!

Pages 96–99

Learn It

1. What is the canon?

   _____.

   How many books are in the Bible canon?

   _____.

How many in the Old Testament?

_____.

The New Testament?

_____.

2. What are two names for the first five books of the Bible?

   _____,

   _____.

   What are the names of these first five books (in order)?

   _____,

   _____,

   _____,

   _____,

   _____.

3. What are the apocrypha?
   a. a heavy metal band from Los Angeles
   b. a collection of ancient books not accepted as part of the Bible canon
   c. the name for the people who copied the Scriptures by hand
   d. the book that Jesus wrote

4. How are the books of the Bible arranged?
   a. topically
   b. alphabetically
   c. alpha-numerically
   d. numerically

Think About It

1. If you wanted to discover the truth about what happened in a particular car accident, which of the following people do you think could describe the accident most accurately? Least accurately? Why?
   a. someone who saw the accident
   b. someone who didn't see the accident
   c. someone who was told about the

accident by someone who saw it

d. someone who was told about the accident by someone who heard about it from someone who saw the accident.

Why do you think it was important to make sure that the books of the New Testament were written by an apostle or someone who worked closely with the apostles?

2. Have you ever felt inspired by God when reading the Bible? What Bible verse or passage were you reading? What did you feel like God inspired you to do?

Do It

1. Have you ever had trouble finding a book in the Bible? Why not solve your problem by memorizing the books in the Bible? Probably the best way to do it is to memorize them topically, much like the way they're broken up on page 97. Start by memorizing the Old Testament historical books. Then the poetic books, and so forth. Before you know it, you'll have the name of every book memorized, in order, and you'll never have trouble finding a book again!

Pages 100–103

Learn It

1. Review the Greatest Story on pages 98–101, then put these Bible stories in the order they occurred:
   _____ a. Saul meets Jesus
   _____ b. The Israelites leave Egypt
   _____ c. Jesus promises to return
   _____ d. God saves Daniel from the lions
   _____ e. The Israelites conquer Canaan
   _____ f. Jesus rises from the dead
   _____ g. Jesus heals the sick
   _____ h. David fights Goliath
   _____ i. God gives Abraham and Sarah a son
   _____ j. Jesus is born in a stable
   _____ k. Jesus dies a horrible death
   _____ l. Adam and Eve sin
   _____ m. Joseph's family come to Egypt

2. What do archaeologists study?
   a. arks
   b. birds
   c. dinosaurs
   d. ancient cultures, artifacts, and peoples

3. Is archaeology confirming or disproving the Bible?

   _____.

   How?

   _____

   _____.

Think About It

1. Have you ever doubted that the Bible was true? Why or why not? What convinced you that it was true?

2. What's your favorite Old Testament story? Your favorite New Testament story? Why are they your favorites?

Do It

1. What do you think things will be like on the day Jesus returns? Revelation 19:11–16 describes what Jesus will look like when he returns to earth. It says he will be a beautiful and powerful rider on a white horse. Read through this passage. Then draw a picture of what you think it will look like on the day Jesus comes riding down out of the sky.

2. Archaeologists are like detectives trying to find the solution to a puzzle. They dig around for clues that will help them get a better understanding of ancient civilizations. Believe it or not, one of the best places to look for clues is in ancient garbage dumps. To the ancient people, things such as broken pottery, old tools, grocery lists, old clothing, and broken weapons were merely trash to get rid of. But to an archaeologist, these items provide precious clues about how people lived in ancient times. By examining these artifacts, archaeologists piece together what the people ate, what they wore, how they wrote, and so on. All of this by simply rooting around in the trash!

You can get a feel for what it's like to be an archaeologist by doing the following activity. Ask a friend or a family member for permission to go through the family's recycling bin over the next month. See if you can find answers to the following questions (Hint: You might want to wear gloves!):

What are their three favorite foods?

What are their two favorite magazines or newspapers?

What is their favorite soft drink? How many gallons do they drink in a month?

Approximately how many boxes of cereal do they consume in a week? A month?

Based on the size of the cans you discover, approximately how many pounds of canned food do they eat in a week? A month?

Based on the envelopes you find, how many letters do they receive in a week? A month?

In addition to the above, make note of any other interesting facts you discover.

Once you are finished with your exploration, write up a brief report that includes your answers to the above questions and a brief description of the family's lifestyle, based on your findings. What surprised you about your explorations? What new facts did you discover about your friend's or relative's family that you didn't know before? Make sure you include these in the report as well. When you're done, share your report with your friend or relative and his or her family. Do they agree with your findings? Why or why not?

Pages 104–107
Learn It

1. What are three reasons why we should read the Bible?

   _____,

   _____,

   _____.

2. Why is it good to memorize Scripture?

   _____

   _____.

3. What's the difference between reading and studying the Bible?

   _____

   _____.

4. How is the Bible like a treasure map?

   _____

   _____.

5. Who or what helps us understand the Bible?
   a. angels on our shoulders
   b. the stars
   c. the Holy Spirit
   d. all of the above

Think About It

1. What are some things in the Bible that you want to know about? How can studying the Bible help you learn about them?

2. What is your favorite Bible verse or passage? Have you ever tried memorizing it? Why or why not? Here's an idea: Make a list of your favorite Bible verses and/or passages and set a goal to memorize one a week over the next three months. Then you'll always have them ready.

Pages 108–111

Learn It

1. Which one of the following is *not* one of the Ten Commandments?
   a. Do unto others as you would have them do unto you
   b. Don't misuse the name of the Lord your God
   c. Don't steal
   d. Don't put any other gods in place of Me
   e. None of the above. They're all part of the Ten Commandments.

2. What is a cross reference?
   a. any place the cross is mentioned in the Bible
   b. a little note beside a verse that points to other verses on the same topic
   c. something on a map that indicates where two roads meet
   d. an angry dictionary

3. What is a concordance used for?

   _____.

4. How is a Bible dictionary different from a normal dictionary?

   _____

   _____.

Do It

1. Take the two week Bible reading challenge! How often do you read the Bible? Once a day? Twice? Once a week? Never? God loves it when we read his Word—the more the better. God speaks to us through the Bible about what he thinks is important, how we can know him, and how we should live. The more we read the Bible, the more things God can teach us.

   The key to developing a regular Bible reading time is to start small and work your way up. If you don't read the Bible regularly, challenge yourself to read it for the next two weeks: choose one of the reading plans on pages 106–107 to follow. Mornings are a great time to read the Bible, right after you pray. Set your alarm clock back five minutes or ask your parents to wake you up five minutes earlier than usual. If mornings don't work for you, try reading the Bible when you get home from school or just before you go to bed. If you already have a regular Bible reading time, try adding an extra chapter or Psalm over the next two weeks. If you're only reading in the New Testament, perhaps you can include an Old Testament reading as well each day.

   You may also want to keep a brief Bible reading journal, noting what you read each day, a key verse in the passage that jumped out at you, what you learned from it, and how you can apply what you learned. Try using these headings: Date; Scripture read; Key verse; Reflections; Ideas for application.

2. *Scripture Guest Book*
   What are some of your all-time favorite Bible verses, passages, or stories? Collecting favorite Bible verses from friends, family, and your own reading and keeping them in a special place is a great way to keep those precious gems close to

your heart. Here's an idea that will help you keep track of the verses that mean the most to you and the people you love. It's called a Scripture Guest Book.

A Scripture Guest Book is similar to a normal guest book except that instead of having people just sign their names, you also have them write down a favorite Scripture verse, passage, or story as well as a brief note explaining why it is special to them. You can either use a normal guest book for this purpose or make your own with headings like the following: Name; Date visited; Favorite Scripture verse, passage, or story; Reason why the verse or passage is special to you; Other comments.

Pages 112–116

Learn It

1. Why does God tell us to study his book?
   a. because there's going to be a test after we die
   b. because he wants to sell more copies
   c. because he gives out prizes to his best students
   d. because it has everything we need for fulfilled, happy, contented lives

2. Does obeying God mean we will never be sad?

   _____.

   Why or why not?

   _____

   _____.

Think About It

1. Why is it important to live out what you learn in the Bible? (Hint: Read James 2:26)

2. Have you ever been "stuck for words" when someone asked you about God or the Bible? What did they ask you? What Bible verse or passage do you think would have helped you in that situation if you had memorized it beforehand?

3. How has reading the Bible helped you to have a better life? What particular lessons, stories, or passages have helped you improve yourself and/or your relationships?

4. What is the best thing you learned about the Bible in this book? Why? How does that truth help you in your life?

Do It

1. When you're doing a Bible study, it is helpful to have a good notebook just for that purpose. Use the following sample Bible study headings as a model to help you create your own Bible study book: Topic; Key verse or passage; Related verses; Questions; Reflections; Ideas for application; Prayer.

   Can't think of a topic? Here are a few to get you started: friends, wisdom, work, sacrifice, apostle, church, prayer, music.

2. Once you've finished memorizing the verses on page 113, try out the following memory verses. Together, they explain how and why we should become Christians. Challenge yourself to memorize these verses in order over the next eight days (one a day) so that you are ready when your friends or family members have questions about how to become a Christian. You can use these verses to walk them through the Bible so they can see what a great thing God did for us by sending Jesus to pay for our sins.

   Romans 3:23; Romans 5:12; Romans 6:23; Romans 5:19; John 3:16; Romans 5:8–9; Romans 10:9–10; Ephesians 2:8–9.

Answers

Pages 88–91
Learn It
1. 1) God's love letter 2) God's instruction manual 3) God's autobiography 4) God's plan.
2. b) more than 40.
3. b) plumber.
4. c) over 1,500 years.
5. b) destroy the copy with the mistake on it.

Pages 92–95
Learn It
1. d) 2,000.
2. The prophecies in the Bible accurately predicted the future. Since only God can know the future, God must have inspired the Bible.
3. b) ancient copies of the Old Testament books found in caves near the Dead Sea.
4. The correct order is: Septuagint, 70 scholars, Vulgate, Jerome, John Wycliffe, Wycliffe Bible, King James Bible, Johann Gutenberg, Gutenberg Bible.

Pages 96–99
Learn It
1. The books that are accepted as Scripture. There are 66 books in the Bible, 39 in the Old Testament and 27 in the New Testament.
2. The Pentateuch and the Law. Genesis, Exodus, Leviticus, Numbers, Deuteronomy.
3. b) a collection of ancient books not accepted as part of the Bible canon.
4. a) topically.

Pages 100–103
Learn It
1. The correct order is: l, i, m, b, e, h, d, j, g, k, f, a, c.
2. d) ancient cultures, artifacts, and peoples.
3. Archaeology is confirming the Bible by making discoveries which show that events, places, and people the Bible describes were real.

Pages 104–107
Learn It
1. 1) To help us understand what God and his book are all about 2) to give us the overall story of God's plan 3) to show us who God is and what he is like.
2. So we know what God wants us to do in different situations.

3. Reading the Bible helps us to learn what God said. Studying the Bible helps us learn why God said it.
4. It helps us find "treasures" in life.
5. c) the Holy Spirit.

Pages 108–111
Learn It
1. a) Do unto others as you would have them do unto you.
2. b) a little note beside a verse that points to other verses on the same topic.
3. Finding verses on a certain topic or finding verses that contain a key word.
4. A Bible Dictionary is different from an ordinary dictionary because it only contains what the Bible says about certain things. It is like a normal dictionary because you can look words up alphabetically and find their meaning.

Pages 112–116
Learn It
1. d) because it has everything we need for fulfilled, happy, contented lives.
2. No, but we will be okay because God will always be with us.

Prayer Is Communication

It's Simple

Talking! Laughing! Singing! Whispering! SHOUTING! Telling secrets. Sharing problems. Chatting. What do these have in common? They're all ways we communicate. And they're all things we can do with God. When we do them with God, they're called *prayer!*

Prayer can be fun! It's simply communicating. Prayer is telling God what's on our hearts—what we feel, think, want, and need. And it's telling him what other people (our family, friends, neighbors, and strangers) need and want, too. It's like having a really good conversation with someone we can trust, and relax and be ourselves with.

Sound simple? It is. It's as simple as talking, laughing, singing, whispering, SHOUTING. . . .

The Big Silence

Imagine waking up one day to discover all sounds are sucked right out of the air and all writing erases itself! No communication! No asking for that special dessert.

No TV (aaagh!). No "I love you" or "Thanks." No asking for help. No songs or stories. No praise or correction. The airwaves are empty. Quiet, huh?

After a while it would feel lonely, too. Unless you learned sign language, no one would know what you're thinking or feeling, what worries you or makes you happy. In fact, no one would know much about you. And you wouldn't know much about them either. No relationship! No friendship!

This silence is what it's like between God and people who don't know him.

The Silence Ends

Once we get to know God, the silence is over! Ending it is pretty simple—we just become God's children (see page 31). Suddenly the communication airwaves between God

The dove represents the Holy Spirit. The Holy Spirit helps us to pray.

all about prayer, and he sent the Holy Spirit to help us pray.

Are you ready to learn about this thing called prayer? Ready to start filling the airwaves between God and you? Dig in for guidelines, answers, information and fun! Here we go!

Kids Say

"God is my friend. . . . I ask him to help me remember how much he loves me." —*Timmy Gill, Florida*

"Kids can talk to God about anything. I do. If I'm feeling bad and don't feel I can tell anybody, I just talk to God about it. It helps me feel better, and he always helps me through things." —*Jacki Bliffen, Florida*

"Kids can pray every day. They can tell God they love him." —*Kristin Roker, Bahamas*

and us start humming! We can build a friendship with him—a Father-child kind of relationship—where the Father accepts us completely, spends time with us, and always listens to us. This Father wants to protect, guide, teach, and take care of us. He wants a great relationship with us, a relationship grown through communication—through prayer! Love—that's what it's all about.

Prayer fills the airwaves between us and our Father God.

But What About…?

Sometimes prayer seems complicated. How do we talk to God when we can't see him? What should we pray about? How does God hear us? What's the right way to pray? Do we have to close our eyes? Does God always answer? There are as many questions as there are people.

God knew we would have questions, so he gave us the answers. He gave us his book, the Bible, to tell us

God's book, the Bible, teaches us about prayer.

Prayer as Relationship

Family Language

Imagine two friends talking. Brad complains, "Dad never plays ball with me! He doesn't even care about what I like to do!"

Tyler asks, "Have you asked him to play ball with you?"

"Naw," Brad answers. "He wants to talk, but I'm not into that!"

Relationships are about loving and understanding each other and doing things together. But they're built by conversation. How will his dad know Brad wants to play ball if Brad never tells him?

It's the same with God and prayer. He wants us to talk to him. He knows everything, but he respects us and our choices. Getting to know God and growing with him isn't automatic—it happens through prayer. We tell God about our friends, how we're doing, what's going on in our lives . . . everything important to us. He loves to know. He loves us more than we can imagine. He wants the best life for us and knows how we'll get it. He'll train us in the skills we need and help us grow into fantastic people!

Since this all happens through prayer, that makes prayer pretty important. It's the foundation, the communication language of God's family.

Prayer Is . . .

Which of these things is not like the others: telephone, map, clothes, party, treehouse, father?

Father is the only person on the list. Father is whom we pray *to*. The others are what prayer is *like*.

Telephone: keeps us in touch with our friends, just as prayer connects us to God.

Map: shows landmarks, danger spots, and the best way to get places. Through prayer, God helps us to see where we're heading and to make the best choices to arrive there safely.

Clothes: cover us and protect us from cold. When we pray, God protects us and keeps us safe.

Party: celebration and fun. Prayer can be a great time of thanking God and celebrating the good things he's done. Enjoy it!

Treehouse: a private place to spend time with a good friend. Prayer is that special place where we spend time with God. We share our secret wishes and thoughts, and we ask God to share his. It's the place where we can really get to know God.

Why did our Father God give us prayer so we could get to know him? Because he loves us to pieces!

Made for Relationship with God

"A father is tender and kind to his children. In the same way, the Lord is tender and kind to those who have respect for him" (Psalm 103:13–14).

"I will be your Father. You will be my sons and daughters" (2 Corinthians 6:18).

"Because you are his children, God sent the Spirit of his Son into our hearts. . . . By his power we call God 'Abba.' Abba means Father" (Galatians 4:6).

"God chose us to belong to Christ before the world was created. . . . He loved us. So he decided long ago to adopt us as his children" (Ephesians 1:4–5).

"How great is the love the Father has given us so freely! Now we can be called children of God. And that's what we really are!" (1 John 3:1).

"Don't worry about anything. Instead, tell God about everything. Ask and pray. Give thanks to him" (Philippians 4:6).

Prayer Gone Bad

In the Beginning

Have you ever received a terrific gift? It works great! You enjoy it for a while. Then it breaks and just doesn't work the same anymore. That's what happened to prayer.

When God made the first people, prayer worked as it was designed to. Adam and Eve had a fantastic relationship with God. They knew they were his deeply loved children. They talked to him about anything. Nothing got in the way of their relationship with their Father.

The Big Mistake

Then Adam and Eve disobeyed God: **Sin!** Everything changed. Suddenly they were afraid of God and no longer felt like his children. Their relationship was broken. They tried to hide and keep secrets from God, and prayer went down the tubes.

People began to think of prayer as a duty, something they had to do to keep from getting into trouble or to stop God from getting angry. They forgot about God's great love. They lost the relation-ship and focused on rules and formulas. They thought, *If I can just do it right, I'll get the answer I want.* Many people even stopped believing prayer would make a difference.

Rules, Not Relationship

It didn't take long for prayer to become something that had nothing to do with relationship with God. People began to treat prayer as a magic formula—if you said the right words, in the right way, at the right time, you could convince God or the "universe" to do something for you. They even developed

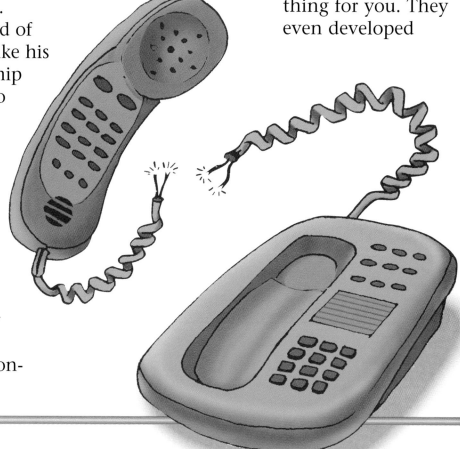

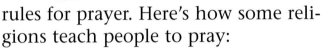
Some religions teach you to "pray" by concentrating on certain sounds and repeating them.

Prayer wheels like this are twirled to release the "mantras" or "prayers."

rules for prayer. Here's how some religions teach people to pray:

Rules Rule: You must pray so many times daily facing a certain direction. Rules tell you where your hands must be, when and what to do with your body—bow, kneel, sit, touch your head to the ground—where to put your feet and fingers, and what words to say for each position.

Words Rule: Certain words "magically" cause things to happen. Just repeat them.

Wheels Rule: Write prayers, or mantras, on paper scrolls. Attach them to wheels and turn them clockwise. This releases kind powers from the mantras and gains you merit or "goodness points." But, look out! Turning the prayer wheel counterclockwise can release bad powers.

You Rule: You're the only "god." Pray to yourself. It's silly to think there's anyone to help.

False Gods Rule: There are all kinds of gods. Some are even people who lived great lives. Use the right words, and they'll act or take your cause to a more important god.

Notice something? None of these "rules" see God as lovingly interested in us. Instead, they say we have to convince him to do something for us against his will. And there's no guarantee he'll do what we ask or even listen to us!

Our Misunderstandings

We might have some of these wrong understandings of prayer. Recognize any of these?
- We repeat the same prayers without thinking about what they mean.
- We must use the "right" words or phrases when talking to God.
- We don't need to pray. We can take care of ourselves, no problem.
- It doesn't matter whether we pray or not—it won't make a difference anyway. God isn't interested in us.

Built for Prayer

God's Design

Question: What exists in the remotest parts of Earth, the smallest town and the biggest city? Answer: Prayer of some kind and respect for God or gods! Why do people believe in God or a "god" and try all sorts of things to communicate with him? Because the desire to pray is built into us.

Any good car has one purpose—to move people around safely and comfortably. Every part of the car—wheels, battery, seats, wipers, transmission—is designed to fulfill that purpose.

Like a car, we're designed for a purpose—to have a relationship with God as our Father. All the parts God built into us—like thoughts, brains, feelings—work toward that purpose. They're all designed to help us communicate naturally with our heavenly Father. It's no wonder prayer is everywhere: It's the key to God's purpose for us!

In fact, it's not just we who are designed for prayer: *Life* works by prayer. God wants us to have the best possible life. That comes out of relationship with him—letting him care for, teach, and protect us—which happens through prayer. Want a great life? Pray!

One of a Kind

You're different from anyone who's ever lived! God had a one-of-a-kind design when he made you. That means you relate to God differently than anyone else does.

Every parent loves all their children. But each child has a different relationship with his or her parents. You like lots of hugs; your sister may not. You may enjoy playing ball with your dad; your brother may prefer doing something else.

It's the same with God. We each relate to him in a way perfectly suited to who we are. God has unique relationships with everyone he made. He loves us all equally. He has a special you-shaped spot in his heart. That means everyone has to develop his or her own relationship with God. Every relationship will be different, but they're all built by spending time with God. What will yours be like?

All Ears

God hears every prayer. He's not limited to one set of ears. He can concentrate on zillions of people at once while holding the universe together with his little finger!

These days computers "multitask" and run several programs at once. A computer sends a shuttle into space, directs its course, regulates oxygen, keeps instruments going, adjusts fuel usage, records astronauts' body temperatures, and much more. All at once! If people can make something that amazing, just think what God can do! He can hear the prayers of every single person at the same time. There's no way you or your prayers could ever get lost or missed. Not only can God hear everyone, he gives each of us his complete, loving, undivided attention.

God is all ears. He's listening to *you!*

God made everyone different. He has one-of-a-kind relationships with each of us.

Did You Know?*

- 88 percent of Americans pray
- 78 percent say prayer is important in daily life
- 63 percent pray often (25 percent pray sometimes)
- 65 percent believe they've had prayers answered specifically
- 79 percent say prayer can speed up recovery from sickness
- 86 percent of teens say they should pray more

*Summary report provided for Lightwave Publishing by the Roper Center, University of Connecticut (Storrs, Conn.), 1997. The report cited findings from the Princeton Survey Research Associates for the Pew Research Center, June 1996 and for the Times-Mirror Company, July 1994; the CBS/*New York Times* Poll, September 1995; Yankelovich Partners Survey for *Time* and Cable News Network, January 1995 and June 1996. Also, "Youthviews," Volume 3, Number 8, April 1995, The George H. Gallup International Institute, Princeton, N. J.

God's Will

Smart Living

With a new video game, the manufacturer's instructions say: "Do not sit on. Do not put in toaster. Do not use in water." Obvious! A video game works best when it's used for what it's made for.

Life is like that. God is not being mean when he tells us to do certain things (be honest, obey our parents, don't steal). He made us, and he made life. He knows how it all works best. These rules are his "manufacturer's instructions" for how life was made to work.

Doing things God's way is just smart living. It makes a fantastic life possible. God gave us an instruction manual (the Bible) to go with our lives so we would know his way. It's easy to obey God when we know that everything he tells us to do is meant to help us have a wonderful life. His will is great! And it's written in the Bible.

Praying for Success

What's God's will got to do with prayer? Everything! Successful praying *is* praying God's will. It's successful because, if God tells us to do something, he'll help us do it. And if he says he'll do something, he will. The Bible says God's will is for us to be honest, be kind, tell people about Jesus, and so on. When we pray for these things, we can trust God to take care of them. The more we agree with God's written will, the Bible, the more he answers our prayers.

The key is to ask for what God wants to give, because we trust his love and know his way is best. Simple.

The Bible doesn't give God's will for everything, such as whether we should try out for the play. When we're not sure about God's will, we can still pray for it. Consider these prayers: "Dear God, my friends are in the play. I want to be in it too. Please make sure I get a role. Amen." Or: "Dear God, my friends are in the play. I'd like to join them. If it's what you want for me, please help me get a role. If not, I know that you know best. In Jesus' name, amen."

Which of these prays for God's will? The second! It makes sense to ask God to answer our prayers his way, not ours. We can pray without fear because we know God loves us. We can trust him to give us what's best.

The Greatest Commandments
(Mark 12:30–31)

Love the Lord your God with all your heart and with all your soul. Love him with all your mind and with all your strength. Love your neighbor as you love yourself.

Cosmic Shopping Channel?

Want list: Best friend. Good grades. New jacket. My own room.

Some people pray as if God is a galactic superstore or a huge, cosmic shopping channel. How well do you know the people on the shopping channels? You don't! That's the problem with treating prayer like a shopping list. The whole reason for prayer is *relationship*.

God isn't a shopping network—he's a person. He wants us to know him, realize his love for us, and ask for things in that context. God enjoys giving good gifts. But he also wants to hear how we feel and what we're thinking. He wants to give us wisdom and help us grow. Why? We're his children! He's our Father. Talk to him from your heart. His answer will be fantastic!

What to Pray

Talk Types

"Guess what happened today!"

"You look great!" "I hope I make the team!" These are all examples of "pleasure" talk. This talk expresses who we are and what's going on in our lives. It's about the daily things that make life interesting and fun. With it, we get to know each other and express our love for each other.

"Did you make your bed?" "I need help with math." "Who's driving?" "Oops! I forgot the garbage!" These are "business" talk things. They have more to do with the nitty-gritty of daily living: chores, schedules, studies, and so on. With this talk, we help everyone do their part and find out who's doing what.

Both talk types are important.

Pleasure Prayers

Like "pleasure" talk, pleasure prayers are about relationship. We tell God how we're doing, what's going on, our hopes and dreams, and our wishes and fears. We take the time to let God in on our lives. And we take time to get to know him.

Pleasure prayers might be:

Family: Thanks for the great time tonight! Please give us a good holiday.

School: Help me do my best in the drama tryouts. Science class was fun today.

Me: I had a great day! Thanks for helping me tell the truth.

Friends: Sarah's very sad—please help her. I'm sorry I hurt Jon's feelings. Please forgive me.

Business Prayers

We need to "talk business" with God too. The Bible tells us to pray for certain things like our leaders, the church, and people who don't know God. God wants us to grow and learn to love others. Part of that involves praying for other people. So we need to take time to pray about the business of Christian living. In these prayers, we agree with God about the things important to him. These are more structured prayers and might be similar each time.

Some business prayers might be:

Family: Please protect our family. Help Mom and Dad make good decisions. Help us get along.

School: Give Miss Wilson wisdom to teach science well. Help Janey know you.

Church: Help Pastor Dan as he preaches. Show us good ways to help people in our community.

Country: Help our political leaders make wise decisions. Keep the police and firefighters safe as they do their jobs.

World: Please keep our missionaries, the Browns, safe and help them tell people about you. Please feed the people who are hungry.

Friends: Help Sandy and I get along. Thanks for helping John get better.

Me: Help me obey you. Please help me understand what I read in the Bible.

Find the following prayer situations in the puzzle below:

- Pray for those who hurt you (Matthew 5:44).
- Pray for workers in the harvest (Matthew 9:38).
- Pray that you won't sin (Matthew 26:41).
- Pray others will do right (2 Corinthians 13:7).
- Pray for God's people (Ephesians 6:18).
- Pray for open doors for God's message (Colossians 4:3).
- Pray for those in authority (1 Timothy 2:1–2).
- Never stop praying (1 Thessalonians 5:17).
- Give thanks no matter what (1 Thessalonians 5:18).
- Pray when in trouble. Sing praises when happy (James 5:13).

Types of Prayers

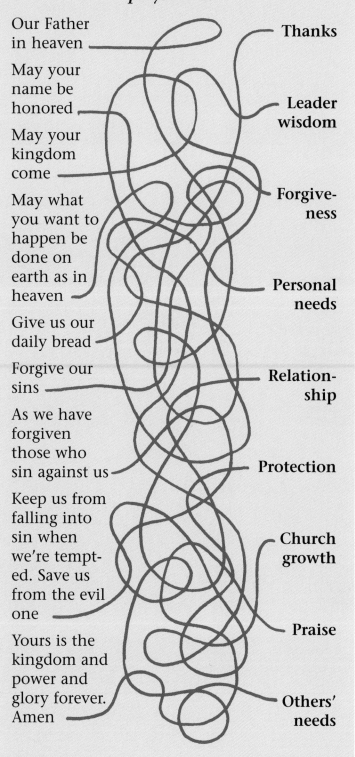

Match the phrase with the kind of prayer it is.

Our Father in heaven

May your name be honored

May your kingdom come

May what you want to happen be done on earth as in heaven

Give us our daily bread

Forgive our sins

As we have forgiven those who sin against us

Keep us from falling into sin when we're tempted. Save us from the evil one

Yours is the kingdom and power and glory forever. Amen

Thanks

Leader wisdom

Forgive-ness

Personal needs

Relation-ship

Protection

Church growth

Praise

Others' needs

A Prayer Pattern

Any guesses who the best pray-er is? Jesus! Jesus loved to pray. Sometimes he even prayed all night! Jesus taught his followers about prayer. He even gave them a pattern prayer that teaches the key things to pray about. You probably know it. It's called "The Lord's Prayer" or "Our Father." Here's what it teaches:

Our Father in heaven: God has a loving Father **relationship** with us. We can relate to him as we do our human fathers.

May your name be honored: We honor God and what he's done. That means **thanking** him for how wonderful and loving he is to us.

May your kingdom come: God's kingdom comes by people getting to know him and obeying him. We pray for God's **church to grow** strong and healthy and for people to become Christians.

May what you want to happen be done on earth as it's done in heaven: We tell God we want his will. We pray **leaders** will have **wisdom** and want God's will.

Give us today our daily bread: We trust God to take care of us. We bring our **personal requests** and needs to him.

Forgive us our sins: None of us do God's will perfectly. So we ask God to **forgive** us and help us grow and become more like he wants us to be.

Just as we also have forgiven those who sin against us: Other people make mistakes. We need to forgive them when they hurt us and pray for **their needs** too.

Keep us from falling into sin when we are tempted. Save us from the evil one: We ask for God's **protection** from bad things and temptations. We ask him to help us choose the right way.

For yours is the kingdom and the power and the glory forever. Amen: We **praise** God because he has the power to answer all these prayers. "Amen" means we know God hears us and answers our prayers.

Public Prayers

Prayer isn't just for our private or family life. Praying with others is important! The church is people (each with a special relationship with God) gathered together to focus on God and his kingdom. Part of doing that is worshiping, praying, and singing together. In *worship* we tell God how wonderful he is. We invite him to work in the church, telling him we want to obey and love him more.

And we pray together. This public prayer is about the needs of the group and God's will being done in the world. When someone is praying out loud, we listen quietly and agree with the prayer. Jesus said, "Suppose two of you on earth agree about anything you ask for. My Father in heaven will do it for you. Where two or three people meet together in my name, I am there with them" (Matthew 18:19–20).

When Do We Pray?

In the Middle of Living

When you hang out with your best friend, when do you talk? Whenever you think of something to say! Think of God as your best friend. You can "hang out" with him all the time. Whenever you think of something to say or ask, go for it!

But let's get specific:

During:	You Might Pray:
Waking up	Thanks for good dreams. Help me be kind today.
Breakfast	Thanks for looking after me and giving me good food.
School	Help me remember what I studied. Bless Miss Jones.
Recess	Thanks for Sandy and for fun! Help John be kind.
Lunch	Please help this food give me energy for sports.
Going home	Help Mr. George drive carefully.
Sports	Please help me learn to dribble. Give Coach Hardy wisdom.
Dinner	Thanks for my great family and Dad's good cooking.
Trouble	Joey got hurt today. Please help him.
Night	What a great day! Thanks. Please give me good dreams.

Get it? Pray anytime, anywhere, about anything—right in the middle of living!

Set-Aside Times

Sometimes special needs come up: your mom has an interview, your sister is sick, or your friend wants to be a Christian. These are great times to pray.

We have other times set aside specifically to spend with God—church, family devotions, Sunday school, or bedtime. These are special times designed to focus on God and communicate with him.

Alone Times

You enjoy being alone with your best friend. That's when you talk about what's important to you and really get to know each other. It's the same with God. When you're alone with him, you can tell him your inner-most feelings, what you like about yourself, and what you want help changing. You can tell him your secret dreams and wishes and ask him about his. Start setting aside five to ten minutes. As you get used to it, increase your time. Soon you'll be having such a good time with your Friend that a half hour passes in a flash! Alone times with God are the special times where you learn to understand his love. It's a great idea to have your Bible handy. When you read it before or after praying, God can use it to teach you and show you what he's like.

You can't grow a close friendship with someone you see once in a while or only when others are around. And you can't grow a close relationship with God if you talk to him occasionally or only at church. He wants a personal, one-of-a-kind friendship with you. That means only you and he can build it!

For Good Private Prayer Times

Choose a time when:
- You're wide awake. (The middle of the night's out!)
- You've done your homework and chores. (Prayer is no excuse to skip chores.)
- You'll have uninterrupted time. (Two minutes before ball practice won't do.)
- There's enough light to read your Bible by. (Although flashlight reading can be fun.)
- No one's going to bother you. (After the first breakfast call is bad timing.)
- There are no distractions. (No TV or music blaring.)
- You're comfortable. (Hanging from monkey bars gets distracting.)

How and Where to Pray

Say It with Your Body

Moses stood. David danced. Solomon raised his hands. Elijah put his head between his knees. Daniel knelt. They were all praying! Our bodies express our feelings. People know we're sad or happy by how we stand or sit. We use our bodies in prayer too. We hold or raise hands, bow our heads, close our eyes. . . . The key is to match our body to our attitude—and be honest about our feelings.

When we're . . .	We might . . .
happy	do a "David" and jump up and down, thanking God
sorry	lay face down
agreeing with others	stand with them or hold their hands
praying intently	kneel or sit with our head bowed
just talking with God	sit in our favorite chair

Say It with Your Tone

The words we choose and how we say them are important too. God loves us. And he is *God*: holy, pure, powerful. So we should pray respectfully. That means being polite, honest, and open. God deserves our honesty and respect. We can tell God how we feel, even if it's negative. But that doesn't mean shouting or being rude if we're angry. No way! We can say how we feel respectfully.

Say It with Others

Listen: You know those times when someone talks about one thing while another talks about something else, and neither listens to the other?

Frustrating! We need to pay attention to what people are saying.

Praying with others is like that. When one person is praying, everyone else should listen. Praying with others means we're saying, "Yes, please answer this prayer." And remember, public prayers are about things that matter to the whole group.

Mean it: Think of singing in church. We don't sing just to make pretty sounds. We're singing and praying to God! We should be paying attention to the words and thinking about their meaning.

Practice: Mealtime prayers at home are a safe place to practice public praying and to learn to pray in front of others. Ask your parents if you can take turns saying the blessing or "grace."

Say It in the "Closet"

Small, dark space. Clothes tickling your cheek. Shoes underfoot. Oh, and an old tennis racket for a seat. Closet prayer! That's not exactly what Jesus had in mind when he told people to go into their closet to pray. He meant, "Don't show off by letting everyone know you're praying." Prayer is about God and us, not about impressing people with how spiritual we are. That's why Jesus told us to pray in private.

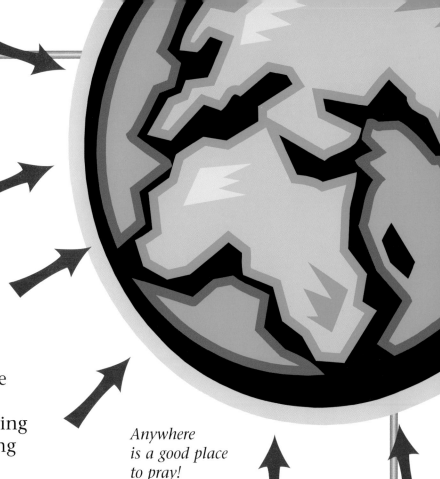

Anywhere is a good place to pray!

There's another good reason for praying in a private place: Concentration! When we talk to someone, we look at their face and eyes. It helps us concentrate on what they're saying and see their reaction to what we say. God isn't with us in a body; he's spirit. He is completely present wherever we are, but we can't see spirit with our physical eyes. So we need to focus on him with our hearts and thoughts. To do this properly, it's best to close our eyes to get rid of physical distractions. As we get to know God through prayer, we'll "see" and "hear" him with our hearts.

Memorized Prayers

Borrow the Right Words

"I pledge allegiance to the flag of the United States of America, and to the republic for which it stands, one nation under God, indivisible, with liberty and justice for all." United States citizens learn these words by heart. They don't have to hunt for words for their promise. Long ago someone carefully chose just the right ones. Thinking about those words tells us what's important to the United States.

Sometimes we can't find the right words for our prayers. How should I pray for God's will? What's the best way to ask God to look after me? How can I pray for my friends to know God's love? When we run into trouble finding the right words, we can "borrow" prayers from others. Some people are good at finding great words for their needs and requests. We can make their prayers our own.

Owned and Unowned Prayers

You probably use memorized prayers already: the Lord's Prayer, "grace" at meals, bedtime prayers like "Now I lay me. . . ." The key is to think about the words you're using as you pray and about the person you're talking to: God! When you focus on the meaning of the words and speak sincerely to God, you make the memorized prayer your own. You're no longer "borrowing" someone else's prayer—you're praying from your heart.

Saying the words without meaning them just wastes words! It's like saying, "That meal was great!" every time you talk to your mom. Are you really talking to her? No, the conversation is meaningless. Memorized prayers work well for the right situations, when we own them and mean them. Otherwise they too become meaningless, unowned prayers.

Choosing Prayers

To make borrowed prayers your own, you'll want to find ones that you like, that mean a lot to you, and that express what you feel or need. Here are some places to look:

- Check out the prayer books some churches use.

- Your parents or friends might have favorite prayers they can teach you.

- Take time to write out your own special prayer—when you've got it just right, memorize and use it.

- One of the best places to look is the Bible. It's chock-full of fantastic prayers—especially in the Psalms. One example is Psalm 23, "The Shepherd's Psalm."

And remember, prayer is about relationship. You have favorite sayings or phrases you use with close friends. Used at the right times, they're fun. But letting them become the main part of your conversation gets pretty silly. The same with prayer. Our relationship is built by speaking from our hearts, telling God how we're doing, what's going on. And that changes from day to day. So should our prayers.

In the Bible, David wrote songs to God. You can borrow his Psalms for your prayers.

Using Scripture to Pray

You can pray Bible verses from memory. Or you can read the verses and go through them one phrase at a time, thinking about each line. What does it mean to you? Is there something you should respond to? What does it say about God? Pray that phrase, adding your own thoughts.

Try using these verses:
When you're worried: John 14:1
When you're afraid: Psalm 23:4
When you've done wrong: 1 John 1:9
When you want something: Psalm 37:4
When you want to praise God:
  Psalm 100:1–2

God's Answers

Yes: *When Jonah ran from God, a big fish swallowed him. He prayed for forgiveness. God said, "Yes!" The fish spit Jonah onto dry land.*

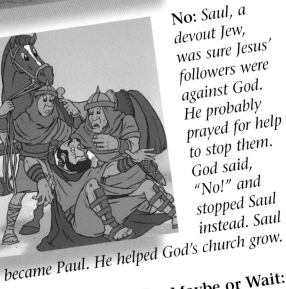

No: *Saul, a devout Jew, was sure Jesus' followers were against God. He probably prayed for help to stop them. God said, "No!" and stopped Saul instead. Saul became Paul. He helped God's church grow.*

Maybe or Wait: *Joseph's brothers sold him as a slave. He probably begged God for help. But God said, "Wait." Much later, God made Joseph the second highest ruler in Egypt! Joseph told his brothers, "You planned to harm me. But God planned it for good!" (Genesis 50:20).*

Preset Answers

Asking to borrow the car when you're twelve always gets a "No" answer. But "Can I do my homework?" gets a "Yes!" "Can I go to Sandy's?" isn't as clear. What's the difference? The first two have preset answers. The third doesn't. Prayers are like that.

"No" Prayers: The Bible tells us what God is like. It's clear God won't do some things. For example, God is love. Asking him for revenge on Jason won't work. Nor will asking to pass exams without studying. The Bible tells us to love our neighbor and to work hard. God won't answer prayers that go against what he says in the Bible.

"Yes" Prayers: Some prayers definitely get a "Yes." They agree with the Bible and who God is, or ask for something God said he'd do. For example, God said he'd provide our needs. So when we pray for them, we know he'll say, "Yes!" When God tells us to do something, he helps us do it. So praying for help to forgive a friend gets a "Yes." These answers are preset! We need to ask and trust God, but when we do, he does what we ask.

"Maybe" or "Wait" Prayers: Then there are the question marks—prayers the Bible doesn't cover, specific requests like "Please help me make the team" or "Please give me a bike for my birthday." The key is to pray

for God's will. Then, whatever the answer, it will be best. We can trust God's love. Sometimes God answers, "Wait." Just like our parents won't let us drive before we have a license, God won't give us what we ask for when we're not ready. "Yes" might harm us.

Remember, we know that God hears *every* prayer. He always answers according to the Bible and what's best for us.

Parenting Answers

God also answers as a parent. The foundation of our relationship with him is being his children. We become God's children when we believe he sent Jesus to die for our sins.

Like our parents, God works to grow our character so we'll have a good life. If we disobey, do our parents talk football? Nope. They talk obedience. If we're fighting, do they take us to the mall? Not likely! They deal with the issue. In the same way, if we're disobeying God or fighting and not forgiving, God works on that. He wants us to obey him and forgive and love everyone like he does. Everything is on hold to deal with that. Then God moves on to deal with our other prayers.

Faith Stories

Start a collection of stories about God's answers to your prayers. You could divide the pages of a notebook down the middle. Write the prayer on one side and the answer on the other. Or just write out the

Jesus prayed for God's will all the time.

whole story. You could also write down family prayers and answers. When answers come, celebrate with Prayer Answer Parties. Soon you'll have a collection of stories that will really encourage your faith!

Whatever answer God gives, it's the right one. We can trust him because he's trustworthy. We can have faith in God because he's faithful—he always does what he says. And remember, God's will for us is the best.

Testing Our Faith

Ready?

Scuba divers test their equipment. Teachers test our knowledge. Why? If the person (or object) isn't ready for the next step—diving or seventh grade—they'll fail. Failure can be discouraging or even dangerous (especially in deep water)!

When it seems like God is silent or saying no to something important, we might doubt and wonder if he hears us. "If he loves me why doesn't he . . . ?" we ask. This could be a test. Whatever it *looks* like, one fact doesn't change: God loves us and does what is best for us. He can always be trusted!

Why the Silence?

God has good reasons for what he does—like growing us to be like Jesus. He could be silent because:

You have to grow into it: You're asking for something you aren't ready for, like playing in a competition before learning the skills.

It might hurt you: You don't understand what would happen if you got what you wanted. Being friends with that cool kid could lead to a bad attitude that hurts you and your family.

God has something better: God says no to making the soccer team so that you can go on an amazing trip.

You need to know where you're at: God stretches you so you can see what your faith is like. When it seems he's not listening, we're tempted to stop trusting. The result? Often the answer doesn't come. But if we keep believing, eventually the answer comes, and our faith grows. Each time we hang on to trust

Prayer Checklist

- Develop your relationship with God by talking to him every day, not just when you want something or have a problem.
- Line up your prayers with who God is. (Don't ask him to be mean!)
- Pray for things the Bible says to pray for.
- Don't pray for what the Bible says *not* to pray for.
- Pray for God to do things according to his will, not yours.
- How is your faith? If it's low, God can increase it (Ephesians 2:8).

- Be thankful. Praise and thanks are important parts of prayer.
- Keep praying. Don't give up. God is always working even when we can't see it.

Don't Forget:

- Sins can come between God and us. Confess any sins (be specific) and ask forgiveness.
- Forgive people who've hurt you. Ask God to help. He understands how much it hurts.

it gets easier—we remember all the times God came through. Tell God your doubts and questions. Ask for help to keep trusting. Remember, it's all about relationship with him.

The Bible Speaks

"You will face all kinds of trouble. When you do, think of it as pure joy. Your faith will be put to the test. You know that when that happens it will produce in you the strength to continue. The strength to keep going must be allowed to finish its work. Then you will be all you should be" (James 1:2–4).

Joseph faced troubles when his brothers sold him.

"We are full of joy even when we suffer. We know that our suffering gives us the strength to go on. The strength to go on produces character. Character produces hope. And hope will never let us down" (Romans 5:3–5).

Listening to God

Walkie-Talkie Prayer

"James, this is Bond. I'm in position. Over." *Sssst.*

"Roger, Bond. Go on 'three.' Over and out!" *Sssst.*

That's walkie-talkie talk. Only one person can talk at a time. You say "over" to tell the other person it's his turn. "Over and out" means you've finished your conversation—kind of like "Amen" at the end of a prayer.

We don't say, "Over," when we pray, but maybe we should! It would remind us to stop talking and *listen.* After all, conversation is a two-way thing.

It takes at least two people, and each person should have a chance to respond. That means we have to stop talking. We can't listen while we talk. We can't get to know someone without listening.

We give God a chance to respond by waiting quietly in his presence. "Be still and know that I am God" (Psalm 46:10). God doesn't speak like we do, so how do we hear him? When we're quiet before God, new thoughts, understanding, wisdom, faith, or even God's peace might come. These things help us understand God's will better.

God Speaks in Many Ways

- ***The Bible:*** God helps us understand a passage or remember a verse that relates to our prayer. We listen by reading, studying, and memorizing God's Word.
- ***Pastors and Christian leaders:*** They've studied the Bible and spent time getting to know God. God can give them wisdom to help us. We should listen to them.
- ***Parents:*** God made our parents responsible for us. He gives them everything they need to help us grow into the people he wants. We need to respect and listen to them.

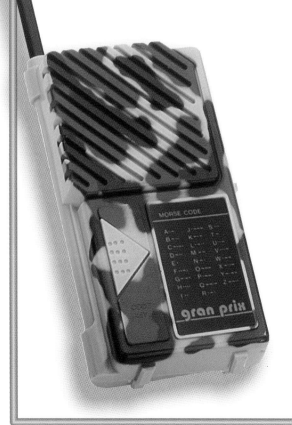

- *Older, wiser Christian friends:* Our friends can pray for us, give us advice, and help us find answers. If their lives show they're following God, their advice is probably good.
- *Life events:* God works everything together for our good. Sometimes, by paying attention to our circumstances, we can learn what God wants for us.
- *Strange events:* In the Bible, God used miracles, visions, dreams, and angels to talk to people! God can speak to us in dozens of ways!

In fact, God can speak anytime, anywhere, in any way he wants. Most of the time, though, he speaks in our hearts and lives in a way that doesn't seem like he's talking at all. But he is. Let's be quiet, ask God to teach us and give us wisdom, read the Bible, and listen every day. We'll find our thoughts going in God's direction—and that's the best for us.

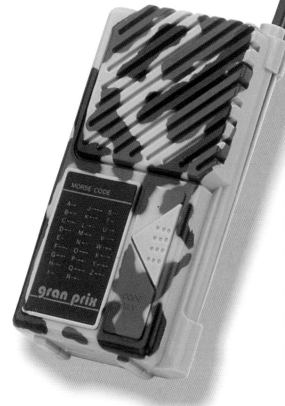

George Washington Carver

As a boy, George prayed for a knife to whittle with. He dreamed of one stuck in a watermelon out in the field. The next day when he looked, there it was! George learned that God hears and answers prayers.

Later, George became a scientist and asked God to show him the wonders of the universe. God said, "No. But I'll show you the wonders of the peanut." George Washington Carver discovered three hundred different products that can be made from peanuts! His discoveries helped the southern states build a whole new economy. All because he believed God cared and answered!

Working with God

Q When we're bad, can we still pray?

A A person can pray at any time for any need. When people do bad things or make mistakes, they need God more than at any other time. When we do something wrong, we need to talk with God about it and admit our wrong. We need to ask him to forgive us and help us learn and grow so that we can do better next time.

God knows we aren't perfect. He wants to give us wisdom and help us change. If we wait until we're good enough to pray, we'll never pray.

Q Why do we have to pray when God already knows what we're going to pray?

A We could never tell God something he doesn't already know. When we pray, we talk to God about the things God and we are doing together. God designed the universe to work a certain way, and prayer is part of his plan. Remember that one of the most important reasons for praying is for the person *praying* to be changed. So when we pray, we find ourselves becoming more of the kind of people that God wants us to be. *We* learn something from *God!*

Also, God wants to have a relationship with us. You wouldn't say,

"Why do I need to talk to my parents? They know what I need already." Asking God to meet our needs is one small part of prayer.

Q If God has it all planned, can we really change his plan by praying for things?

A No one can see how their prayers affect God. We know God is in control. We also know God hears and cares about our prayers and answers them. God could take care of everything without our prayers, but prayer is his plan.

God wants his people to be coworkers with him in this world. We work with him. Part of that involves prayer. Our prayers are part of the way God's work will get done. The Bible tells us repeatedly that our prayers make a difference.

Nothing takes God by surprise. He knows everything, even the future. Also, remember the main reason for praying—to get to know God better and let him teach and care for us.

Q How does God answer our prayers?

A In many ways. God is all-powerful. He can use anything he wants to work out his plans. One of the ways he answers prayer is by using other people. For example, God often uses doctors to bring healing. He uses generous Christians to give money to people in need, in answer to their prayers.

God will often give us wisdom and teach us in order to answer prayer. We may ask for more money. God may answer by helping us learn how to use what we have more carefully. Sometimes God uses angels to do miracles or intervene in some invisible way. He also uses processes and natural forces of nature.

And almost always, God changes our hearts when we pray. He works inside us to make us more like Christ in the way we think, talk, and behave.

Adapted from *107 Questions Children Ask About Prayer*, Tyndale House Publishers, 1998. Used by permission.

Payoff!

Okay, you're praying. You're getting to know God and growing more like Jesus. What now? This is where it all comes together. God built us for prayer. Life works by prayer. Prayer brings the payoff—a great life!

Think—what you *really* want probably includes friends, a great family, fun, happiness, being loved and accepted, feeling safe, having your needs met, and doing what you love—what God created you to do. God has given us the ability to know and learn from him so our lives can be the best. Prayer makes it happen. Oh, not all at once. At first prayer may not seem like everything we've said. But if you keep praying, it will.

God knows how to do life well! And he loves giving good gifts. That means he enjoys doing things for us and helping us grow. When we know this without doubt, prayer becomes exciting and wonderful. The result? We want to pray more, which shows us God's love more, which gets us even more excited about praying!

A good prayer life teaches us God is love. He always:

- accepts, listens to, and wants to be with us
- helps in tough times, is there for us—is available
- believes in, trusts, and challenges us—gives us responsibility knowing we can do it
- forgives, corrects, and guides us—keeps us on track for his awesome plan
- laughs and cries with us—accepts our emotions
- provides for our needs
- shares his joy of life with us

What more could we want? Growing in prayer is growing with God. Growing with God is growing in life. God and his love never change. We can count on him!

Questions and Activities

Pages 126–129

Learn It

1. Which of these things *can't* we do when we pray?
    a. sing
    b. laugh
    c. shout
    d. whisper
    e. we can do all of the above when we pray

2. Which of the following is prayer *not* like?
    a. a telephone
    b. a map
    c. clothing
    d. television

Think About It

1. Why is there silence between some people and God? How can they end this silence?

2. Have you ever lost contact with a friend because he or she moved away? How did the lack of communication affect your relationship with him or her? Were you able to resume contact again? How did that affect your relationship?

3. Have you ever felt like you've "lost contact" with God? How did the lack of communication affect your relationship with God? How did you (or how can you) restore contact with God again?

4. How are your relationships with people built? How is this similar to the way your relationship with God is built? How is it different?

Pages 130–133

Learn It

1. What made prayer "go bad"?

    _____

    _____.

    What were the results of this break in communication between God and his people?

    _____

    _____.

2. Why do people everywhere believe in God or a "god" and try to communicate with him or her?

    _____

    _____.

Think About It

1. Read through the misunderstandings about prayer at the bottom of page 131. Have you ever struggled with any of these? Which ones? What are three things that you've read so far about prayer that have improved your understanding of it?

2. Think about your relationship with God. How is it different from your parents' relationship with God? Your friends'? Your siblings'? How is it the same?

Play It

1. In this section you learned about how sin disrupted the connection between people and God, just like a

storm sometimes knocks out phone or power lines. The following is a list of specific sins that disrupt our ability to communicate with God. Can you figure out how to fix each break in the line so you can get through to God? Look up the verses beside each problem and see if you can figure out the solution.

ANGER

Solution: _____
(James 1:19–20)

UNFORGIVENESS

Solution: _____
(Matthew 6:14–15; 18:21–22)

IGNORANCE

Solution: _____
(Proverbs 9:10; 18:15)

PRIDE

Solution: _____
(Proverbs 11:2; James 4:10)

SELFISHNESS

Solution: _____
(1 Timothy 6:18–19)

GREED

Solution: _____
(Matthew 6:33; Luke 12:15)

JEALOUSY

Solution: _____
(Philippians 4:11–13)

IMPURITY

Solution: _____
(Philippians 4:8)

HATRED

Solution: _____
(1 Peter 4:8)

Pages 134–137

Learn It

1. God gives us rules for how we should live because:
   a. he wants to make life miserable for us
   b. he's gone mad with power
   c. he created life and he knows how it works best
   d. he had nothing better to do

2. What is the key to getting what we ask for in prayer?

   _____

   _____.

3. In which of the following situations might it be appropriate to send a business letter to someone? A personal letter?
   a. to ask someone to marry you
   b. to order a new book
   c. to request information on a new product or service
   d. to find out what your friend has been up to for the past month

4. In which of the following situations might it be appropriate to pray a business prayer to God? A pleasure prayer?
   a. when your aunt is sick with cancer
   b. when you wake up and see the sun shining through your window
   c. when someone you love is in danger
   d. when you receive an "A" on a test

Think About It

1. How would you feel if the only time your friends talked to you was when they needed things? Why is it not good to talk to God only when you need something? Have you ever done this? Is it ever okay to ask God for things? What kinds of things should we ask for?

2. What are a couple of business prayers you can pray this week? A couple of pleasure prayers?

Do It

1. Write a "pleasure prayer" letter to God thanking him for a family member, a friend, a pet, or an experience you really enjoyed. Write it as if you're telling a friend all about who the person is or what the experience was and why you're thankful for it. Once you've completed your letter, put it in an envelope addressed to God and tuck it into your Bible as a reminder of God's goodness to you.

Pages 138–141

Learn It

1. Why did Jesus give us the Lord's Prayer?

_____
_____.

2. Why is it important to pray with others?

_____
_____.

3. During which of the following times should you *not* pray?
   a. when you wake up
   b. at recess
   c. during sports
   d. at supper time
   e. none of the above, we can pray any time we want

4. Why is it important to set aside time to be alone with God?

_____
_____.

Think About It

1. List five things that will help your personal prayer times go better.

_____,
_____,
_____,
_____,
_____.

2. Some people are afraid to pray in front of others. Why do you think this is? How do you feel about praying in front of others? What are some ways you can feel more comfortable about doing this? What are some ways you can help others feel more comfortable about doing this?

Do It

1. The Lord's Prayer is a good prayer to memorize because it gives us a pattern for how all of our prayers should be said. Take 10–15 minutes to memorize the Lord's Prayer now. Start with one line and keep adding the rest until you have the whole thing memorized. You can either pray it each day as part of your daily time with God or simply use it as a model for your own prayers.

The Lord's Prayer

"Our Father in heaven, may your name be honored. May your kingdom come. May what you want to happen be done on earth as it is done in heaven. Give us today our daily bread. Forgive us our sins, just as we also have forgiven those who sin against us. Keep us from falling into sin when we are tempted. Save us from the evil one. For yours is the kingdom and the power and the glory forever. Amen." (Matthew 6:9–13)

2. Take the two week prayer challenge! How often do you pray? Once a day? Twice? Once a week? Never? God loves it when we talk to him in prayer: the more the better. Don't worry, God isn't sitting up in heaven with a giant stopwatch judging us on how long or how short our prayers are. He simply wants us to keep in constant contact with him each day. But the longer we spend in prayer, the more things we can tell God, and the more things he can tell us.

Just like Bible reading, the key to developing a regular prayer time is to start small and work your way up. If you don't pray regularly, try starting with two to five minutes a day. Mornings are a great time to pray. For the next two weeks, set your alarm clock back five minutes or ask your parents to wake you up five minutes earlier than usual. If mornings don't work for you, try praying just before you go to bed. But be careful: don't fall asleep until you're finished!

If you already have a regular prayer time, try adding an extra five minutes over the next two weeks.

During your two week prayer challenge, keep a brief prayer journal like the sample page provided, noting what you prayed about each day. Then keep your eyes and ears open for God's answers!

Sample Prayer Journal

Date: _____

Prayer:

_____

_____

_____

_____

_____ .

Why this issue/person is important to me:

_____

_____

_____

_____

_____

Date prayer was answered:

_____ .

How God answered my prayer:

_____

_____

_____

_____ .

Learn It

1. What is the key to using your body in prayer?

   _____

   _____.

2. Which of the following is not an appropriate posture for prayer?
   a. sitting
   b. standing
   c. kneeling
   d. hanging upside down from the monkey bars
   e. all of the above are appropriate postures for prayer

3. Why is the tone of your prayers important?

   _____

   _____.

4. What are three things to remember when praying with others?

   _____,

   _____,

   _____.

5. Why did Jesus tell us to pray in private?

   _____

   _____.

6. What are two benefits to using memorized prayers?

   _____,

   _____.

   What is one pitfall?

   _____.

7. Where are three good places to find written prayers?

   _____,

   _____,

   _____.

Think About It

1. What are three situations when it might be appropriate to pray in public?

2. Think about some of the memorized prayers you use, even if it's what you say before you eat. What does each prayer really mean?

Do It

1. The book of Psalms is really the "prayer book" of the Bible. It is a collection of prayers and songs written to God by David, Solomon, and other authors. Each Psalm either:
   1) celebrates a different aspect of God's nature or character (Psalm 104)
   2) asks God for help (Psalm 80)
   3) gives thanks to God (Psalm 40)
   4) simply expresses the writer's love for God (Psalm 27).

   Reading and praying through the Psalms is a great way to learn how people in ancient times prayed to God and how we should pray to him today. Some famous Psalms you may want to read, pray through, and possibly memorize are Psalms 1, 8, 23, 37, 47, 97, 98, and 139. Read through the Psalms and pick your own favorites.

   But don't stop there. Why not try and write your own psalm to God? It can do any of the four things that we said psalms do above. Your psalm can be short like Psalm 23 or longer like Psalm 139, depending on how much you want to include. To be like one of the original psalms, it should include three or four main parts:

1) An introduction where you explain the purpose of your psalm.
2) A section that describes the aspect of God's character or nature you are celebrating; the thing, person, or incident you are thankful for; or the problem you need help with.
3) If your psalm is a call for help, the next part should detail how you want God to help you.
4) A closing that includes a final word of praise for God's love and mercy to you.

Once you've completed your psalm, keep it in your Bible or some other place so it is always close at hand. Pray through it whenever the situation is appropriate. You may even want to memorize it, share it with others, or make it the beginning of your own book of psalms, a collection of your prayers to God.

Pages 146–149

Learn It

1. What kinds of prayers are guaranteed to get a "No" from God?

_____

_____.

What kinds of prayers are more likely to get a "Yes"?

_____

_____.

2. Which of the following is *not* a reason why God would respond to your prayers with silence?
   a. he didn't hear you
   b. he has something better for you
   c. what you're asking for may hurt you

d. you're asking for something you aren't ready for

Think About It

1. In what ways is God like a parent to you? In what ways is God different from your parents?

2. Have you ever felt like God was being silent in response to your prayers? If so, why do you think that was? Look at the reasons given for God's silence on page 148. Which of these reasons most likely explains your situation? What can you change about your prayers so that you receive an answer from God?

Do It

1. Take a look at the prayer checklist on page 149. To help you remember some of these points, see if you can come up with six things you should remember about prayer that begin with the letters "P," "R," "A," "Y," "E," "R." For example, the "P" could stand for praise. Once you've created your list, make a bookmark out of a strip of paper and write your prayer reminder list on it. Keep it in your Bible to help you remember how to pray.

Pages 150–154

Learn It

1. Prayer involves both

_____,

_____.

2. Why is it important to listen to God during prayer?

_____

_____.

3. List five ways God speaks to us:

_____,

_____,

_____,

_____,

_____.

Think About It

1. Have you ever felt that God was speaking to you? How did he speak to you? What was he saying? How did you know it was God?

2. What is your favorite thing you learned about prayer in this book? How does it change the way you pray?

Do It

1. Every Christian has at least one faith story to tell—an incident where God answered your prayers or intervened in your life in some sort of extraordinary way. What are some of your faith stories? Sit down with a notebook and ask God to bring some of your faith stories to mind. Jot down the following details about each story:

Date: _____

Circumstances:

_____

_____

_____.

My Thoughts and Prayers:

_____

_____

_____.

Verses that helped me:

_____

_____

_____.

God's Answers:

_____

_____

_____.

Lesson(s) learned:

_____

_____

_____

_____.

Once you begin compiling your list of faith stories, look for opportunities to share them with others. For example, if one of your friends is struggling with worry, share a story about a time when you were tempted to worry but chose to put your faith in God instead. Tell him or her how this event helped you deal with the situation and how God showed himself to be faithful.

ANSWERS

Pages 126–129
Learn It
1. e) we can do all of the above when we pray.
2. d) television.

Pages 130–133
Learn It
1. Sin. We lost contact with God.
2. Because God built the desire to pray right into us.

Play It
1. Have patience.
2. Forgive others.
3. Gain knowledge and wisdom.
4. Make yourself humble before God and others.
5. Be generous.
6. Seek God first above all things.
7. Be content.
8. Dwell on good things only.
9. Love others.

Pages 134–137
Learn It
1. c) he created life and he knows how it works best.
2. Praying according to God's will.
3. Business letter: b and c; Pleasure letter: a and d.
4. Business prayer: a and c; Pleasure prayer: b and d.

Pages 138–141
Learn It
1. To show us how we should pray.
2. To bring the needs of the group and the needs of the world before God.
3. e) none of the above, we can pray any time we want.
4. It's the best way to develop your relationship with God.

Pages 142–145
Learn It
1. To match your body posture with your attitude.
2. e) all are appropriate. We can pray anytime, anywhere, about anything.
3. Because it is important to show respect for God.
4. 1) Listen 2) Mean it 3) Practice.
5. So that we wouldn't be tempted to show off how well we can pray.

6. Benefits: 1) They give us the right words when we can't find them on our own 2) They help us pray God's will. Pitfall: We might just repeat the words of the prayer without meaning them.
7. 1) Prayer books 2) Parents or friends 3) the Bible.

Pages 146–149
Learn It
1. Prayers that go against his will get a no. Prayers that go along with God's will get a yes.
2. a) he didn't hear you.

Pages 150–154
Learn It
1. 1) Talking 2) Listening.
2. Because he has things he wants to tell us.
3. 1) The Bible 2) Pastors and Christian leaders 3) Parents 4) Older, wiser Christian friends 5) Life events 6) Strange events.

Welcome to the Family!

Heritage
Builders

Helping You Build a Family of Faith

We hope you've enjoyed this book. Heritage Builders was founded in 1995 by three fathers with a passion for the next generation. As a new ministry of Focus on the Family, Heritage Builders strives to equip, train, and motivate parents to become intentional about building a strong spiritual heritage.

It's quite a challenge for busy parents to find ways to build a spiritual foundation for their families—especially in a way they enjoy and understand. Through activities and participation, children can learn biblical truth in a way they can understand, enjoy—and *remember.*

Passing along a heritage of Christian faith to your family is a parent's highest calling. Heritage Builders' goal is to encourage and empower you in this great mission with practical resources and inspiring ideas that really work— and help your children develop a lasting love for God.

***

How To Reach Us

For more information, visit our Heritage Builders Web site! Log on to **www.heritagebuilders.com** to discover new resources, sample activities, and ideas to help you pass on a spiritual heritage. To request any of these resources, simply call Focus on the Family at 1-800-A-FAMILY (1-800-232-6459) or in Canada, call 1-800-661-9800. Or send your request to Focus on the Family, Colorado Springs, CO 80995. In Canada, write Focus on the Family, P.O. Box 9800, Stn. Terminal, Vancouver, B.C. V6B 4G3

To learn more about Focus on the Family or to find out if there is an associate office in your country, please visit www. family.org

We'd love to hear from you!

Try These Heritage Builders Resources!

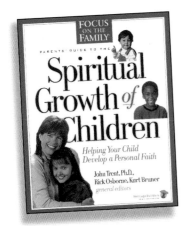

Parents' Guide to the Spiritual Growth of Children

Building a foundation of faith in your children can be easy—and fun!—with help from the *Parents' Guide to the Spiritual Growth of Children*. Through simple and practical advice, this comprehensive guide shows you how to build a spiritual training plan for your family and it explains what to teach your children at different ages.

My Time With God

Send your child on an amazing adventure—a self-guided tour through God's Word! *My Time With God* shows your 8 to 12-year-old how to get to know God regularly in exciting ways. Through 150 days' worth of fun facts and mind-boggling trivia, prayer starters, and interesting questions, your child will discover how awesome God really is!

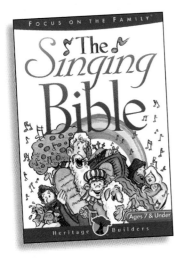

The Singing Bible

Children ages 2 to 7 will love *The Singing Bible*, which sets the Bible to music with over 50 original, sing-along songs! New from Heritage Builders, *The Singing Bible* walks your child through the Old and New Testament Scripture. Introduce Adam and Eve in the Garden, the Ten Commandments, Jonah and the Whale, the Lord's Prayer, and many other biblical characters and facts in this four-cassette collection of songs that will have kids singing along! Memorable lyrics, tongue twisters, and an energetic narrator to guide them makes understanding the Bible an exciting journey. Fun and fast-paced, *The Singing Bible* is perfect for listening and learning!

Heritage Builders™
Helping You Build a Family of Faith

Mealtime Moments

Make your family's time around the dinner table meaningful with *Mealtime Moments*, a book that brings you great discussion starters and activities for teaching your children about your faith. Kids will have fun getting involved with games, trivia questions, and theme nights, all based on spiritually sound ideas. Perfect for the whole family!

Joy Ride!

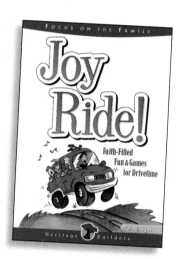

When you think of all the time kids spend in the car, it makes sense to use the time to teach lasting spiritual lessons along the way. *Joy Ride!* is a fun and challenging activity book that helps parents blend biblical principles into everyday life. Games, puzzles, Bible-quiz questions, and discussion starters give parents fun ways to get the whole family involved in talking and thinking about their faith. Make the most of your time together on the road with this fun, inspiring guide. Small enough to fit into a glove compartment, it's great for vacations *and* local trips!

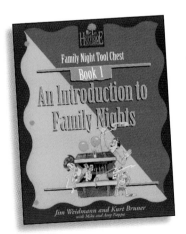

An Introduction to Family Nights

Make devotions something your children will *never* forget when you involve them in "family nights"—an ideal way to bring fun and spiritual growth together on a weekly basis. *An Introduction to Family Nights* delivers 12 weeks' worth of tried-and-tested ideas, object lessons, and activities for helping kids learn how to tame the tongue, resist temptation, be obedient, and much more!

Heritage Builders
Helping You Build a Family of Faith

Every family has a heritage—a spiritual, emotional, and social legacy passed from one generation to the next. There are four main areas we at Heritage Builders recommend parents consider as they plan to pass their faith to their children:

Family Fragrance

Every family's home has a fragrance. Heritage Builders encourages parents to create a home environment that fosters a sweet, Christ-centered AROMA of love through Affection, Respect, Order, Merriment, and Affirmation.

Family Traditions

Whether you pass down stories, beliefs, and/or customs, traditions can help you establish a special identity for your family. Heritage Builders encourages parents to set special "milestones" for their children to help guide them and move them through their spiritual development.

Family Compass

Parents have the unique task of setting standards for normal, healthy living through their attitudes, actions, and beliefs. Heritage Builders encourages parents to give their children the moral navigation tools they need to succeed on the roads of life.

Family Moments

Creating special, teachable moments with their children is one of a parent's most precious and sometimes, most difficult responsibilities. Heritage Builders encourages parents to capture little moments throughout the day to teach and impress values, beliefs, and biblical principles onto their children.

We look forward to standing alongside you as you seek to impart the Lord's care and wisdom onto the next generation—onto your children.

Heritage Builders™
Helping You Build a Family of Faith

building Christian faith in families

Lightwave Publishing is one of North America's leading developers of quality resources that encourage, assist, and equip parents to build Christian faith in their families. Lightwave's products help parents answer their children's questions about the Christian faith; teach them how to make church, Sunday school, and Bible reading more meaningful for their children; provide parents with pointers on teaching their children to pray; and much, much more.

Lightwave, together with its various publishing and ministry partners, such as Focus on the Family, has been successfully producing innovative books, music, and games since 1984. Some of its more recent products include the *Parents' Guide to the Spiritual Growth of Children*, *Joy Ride!*, and *My Time With God*.

Lightwave also has a fun kids' web site and an Internet-based newsletter called *Tips and Tools for Spiritual Parenting*. For more information and a complete list of Lightwave products, please visit: **www.lightwavepublishing.com**.